BRIEF SOJOURN IN YOUR NATIVE LAND

Sydney's *huaqiao* and their links with south China

by

Michael Williams

BRIEF SOJOURN IN YOUR NATIVE LAND

This work originated as a Master of Letters thesis, UNE, 1998.

First edition. January 17, 2025.

ISBN: 978-1-7635605-3-6

Chidestudy

Written by Michael Williams.

Published by *ChideStudy Press*
For inquires or to order copies email:
ChidestudyPress@gmail.com
Website: chidestudypress.com.au

Press

Preface

The initial research for this book was done in the late 1990s as part of a Master of Letters with the University of New England under the excellent supervision of Dr Janis Wilton. I was still working at the time (by a lucky coincidence in the same building as Australian National Archives in the pre-digitalisation era) but was able to include research in both Sydney and the Pearl River Delta. This work later became the basis for much expanded research in the Pearl River Delta district of Long Du and also Hawaii and San Francisco which was published as *Returning Home with Glory* (HKU Press, 2019). As a result, this work was never published. Recently I dusted it off and on rereading, I saw that with minimal updating it still has much to offer. I hope readers will agree.

One aspect of this work was my making connections with many in the Sydney Chinese Australian community who in the nature of things were manly of Zhongshan origin (read further to find out what this means). It was only in the last few years that I learned Mavis Yen at the time I was researching was also living in Sydney in a very near suburb and interviewing for her proposed work. A work only published after her death by her daughter and son-in-law as *South Flows the Pearl* (University of Sydney Press, 2022). How we missed each other I do not know but her wonderful work of oral history closely parallels both this work and *Returning Home with Glory*.

The overall aim of publishing this work is to make academic work more widely available to the general public. Hence all reference footnotes are now endnotes, there are more images and of course it is cheaper. The main text is the same with minor corrections and updates. While an addition Appendix VI notes the research of the last 20 years, there is no real attempt to integrate this research into this text beyond the occasional comment or more recent reference.

CONTENTS

Map

List of Charts

"We hope that your brief sojourn in your native land will be pleasurable and beneficial to your health, and that you will be granted a safe return to your adopted country."

Gundagai, January 9th, 1903

INTRODUCTION
'An Australian citizen apparently'

In the district of Zhongshan (中山), in the south China province of Guangdong, in a small village surrounded by rice fields, sits a rusting 'Ajax' safe bearing the seal 'Anthony Hordern & Sons Ltd. Sydney'.* In a nearby village, the local clinic is run by a doctor who recalls the original clinic established by her father with money earned from his Wollongong store.[1] Displayed in a small district museum nearby is a medal awarded by Sun Yat-sen to an Australian resident for services to the Republic of China. Services that included collecting donations from other Australian residents to purchase aeroplanes for the Republic of China's air force.[2]

What is the connection between such objects, these people, their villages and Australia? They are part of a relationship which puzzled Department of 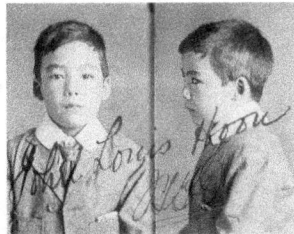 Immigration officials when, in 1955, they noted on the file

---

* See Map, Chapter 1, and Figure 4, Chapter 2. For a discussion of Chinese romanisation, see Appendix I.

of Sydney born John Louie Hoon, whose parents, one born in Australia, the other in south China, had both lived and died in Sydney, that he was 'an Australian citizen apparently'.[3]

From 1901 until well into the second half of the twentieth century, during the height of the White Australia policy, thousands of people of Chinese birth not only lived in Australia but maintained extensive links with their families and villages in south China. Here we will examine the history of that generation of Sydney residents of Chinese origin who lived during the first half of the twentieth century, with particular attention being paid to those whose origin was the district of Zhongshan.♣[4]

Writings on the Chinese in Australia up to the end of the 20th century can be broadly divided into two categories.♦ The first includes studies on the origins and development of race relations and the administration of the White Australia Policy that discuss the history of the Chinese in Australia as 'victims' or 'antagonists' within these issues. The second

---

♣ See Map, Chapter 1. Long known as Heangshan (Xiangshan, 香山), its name was changed to Zhongshan in 1925 in honour of its favourite son, Sun Yat-sen.

♦ Much research has been done in the 20 years since this was first written, a brief summary can be found in Appendix VI.

category of writings on the Chinese in Australia are regional and general histories which discuss the Chinese in their own terms, though sometimes only as an extension of Australia's immigration history. Additionally, there are studies on related topics such as the history of labour importation from China, Australian/China trade relations, biographies of individual Australian-Chinese and studies of the 'overseas Chinese'. This last area of research is the study of what has more recently become known as the 'Chinese diaspora'.

The first 'White Australia Policy' study used parliamentary debates and contemporary newspaper sources to look at the thinking behind the laws and attitudes that characterised this policy.[5] In this study Chinese people were alluded to only in so far as their presence and the reactions they invoked provided insight into Australian policies and attitudes. Subsequent studies, using the records of the administration of the Immigration Act, began to reveal more about how the Chinese community responded to these restrictions but little about their own intentions.[6] Further research of the White Australia Policy's origins, including a recent study of the international pressures placed on Australia because of this policy, also throw only an indirect light on the history of the Chinese in Australia.[7]

Studies on the broader issue of racism have compared the restrictive immigration histories of Australia and the United States to reveal more about the Chinese in Australia. [8] However, despite the range of sources used (only rarely are these Chinese), such studies continue to give a restricted view of the history of the Chinese in Australia by leaving the impression that the Chinese existed only to inspire racial hostility and the White Australia Policy. Studies around the same that used sociological approaches and statistical data did begin to ask questions about how the Chinese lived in Australia, how they responded in their own terms to racial hostility and the White Australia Policy, and how they survived and adapted, not only as immigrants, but as members of the broader society. [9] The first truly historical study of the Chinese in Australia used Chinese language newspapers and the records of Chinese organisations for the first time, as well as sources such as the 'Royal Commission on alleged Chinese Gambling.' [10] This provided a history of Chinese Australians not only as they dealt with the White Australia policy, but also how they conducted business, religion, education, family life and politics. [11]

A limitation of all these writings is that they generally only deal with residents of Sydney and Melbourne or perhaps NSW and Victoria. A number of studies do go beyond Sydney and Melbourne, such as Rolls, who unfortunately uses much unsourced material, and Jupp, who ensures something is said about Chinese migrants in every State.[12] Two oral histories also range nationally. Loh's investigation of the treatment by the defence forces of Chinese-Australians reveals new insights into their history through revealing details of family life and the personal impact of prejudice.* Giese also uses oral history techniques to ask who are Chinese-Australians?[13]

Research into the pre-gold rush and gold rush periods provides valuable information about the origins of the Chinese in Australia. Pre-gold rush Chinese people were usually contracted labourers and older studies on this topic referred to Australia only briefly. More recent studies, however, have examined the history of Chinese indenture and labour importation in Australia.[14] For the gold rush period, researchers have used contemporary accounts in English to examine the origins of hostility to Chinese miners as well as the interaction between them and other miners. The difficulty of providing a Chinese perspective from largely European sources is acknowledged but again

---

* At the time of writing, I was not aware of the more substantial body of work by Morah Loh who was well ahead of most researchers at this time. Unfortunately, most of her work was in local publications now out of print and is difficult to find. See Appendix VI for a partial list.

Chinese people tend to be presented merely as the victims of European hostility.[15]

Works of regional Australian Chinese history dealing with Cairns, Perth, Darwin, Sydney and northern NSW are useful for the diversity of experiences that they reveal. The Chinese community of Cairns, for example, is seen to have been more tolerated by Europeans than Chinese communities elsewhere due to their greater economic strength.[16] Darwin, with its proportionally larger Chinese population, has features not seen in histories based solely on Sydney or Melbourne.[17] Research on the Chinese of Western Australia concludes that they were more isolated and scattered than elsewhere and so consequently had a very different history to those in the 'Eastern States'.[18] The most recent study of Sydney Chinese, using a wider range of sources than has been used previously, shows a community more integrated into the general life of the city than previous studies revealed.[19] Finally, oral history research into the small towns of northern NSW reveals not only another variation on the theme of the Chinese in Australia in its discussion of the family stores networks of the region, but for the first time reveals in detail the role of the continuing links with the home villages for people of Chinese origin in Australia.[20]

Other studies touching upon aspects of the Chinese in Australia include a small number of biographies of Chinese-Australians and some studies of Australian-China trade.[21] The biographies have not generally been able to develop the context in which such men lived. While in the trade studies the details of how trade was carried out and the role of Chinese communities in Sydney, Melbourne or elsewhere are not touched upon. [22] Chinese firms owned by businessmen who first developed their business skills operating stores in Sydney before founding large companies in Hong Kong and Shanghai have also been studied but surprisingly little has been revealed about the Australian contribution.[23]

The research referred to above concerns the history of the Chinese in Australia but little is said in any of these studies concerning the principal context to this history, that is, the 'overseas Chinese'. Many books have been written about the Chinese communities of the *Nanyang* (South East Asia) but these make few references to Chinese migration to Australia.[24]

In the late 1980s, the first studies of the 'overseas Chinese' as such began in China and North America.[25] These studies have begun to reveal much that could be characterised as a 'Chinese migrant pattern'. The most interesting study

7

proceeded from a joint Chinese/United States project concerning Taishan immigrants to the United States. [26] Canada has also produced a number of studies that focus particularly on a single lineage. As well, and a detailed study has been made of a Hong Kong village and its emigrants to Britain.[27]

Research in China itself has focused either on the evaluation of various types of sources, such as the clan records, tomb inscriptions, clan and district publications, or on detailed analysis of the uses remittances were put to and the impact generally of overseas Chinese on the development of their villages and districts of origin. The perspective of Chinese scholars is very much that the overseas Chinese represent a social phenomena within China's history and society and so their role in other countries is an aspect of China's history, a history that stretches back to the 12th century and continues to the present day.[28] These studies make few references to Australia although it is recognised that, after the *Nanyang* and North America, Chinese people emigrated most often to Australia. This was a very distant third, however, and no Chinese research has been directed to Australia specifically.[29]

Districts of origin

An element which neither North American and Chinese studies, nor Australian regional studies in have focused on, is the role of the district of origin. As one sinologist has put it, 'We need to further disaggregate the Australian-China communities into their various ethnic and sub-ethnic groups.' Additionally, 'We need to place the Australian material into a Chinese cultural context. … the emigrant areas of south-east China.'[30] This work attempts to place the history of the generation under discussion into the context of south China and to take some tentative steps in the direction of disaggregation along the lines of districts of origin.*

A focus on the districts of origin also emphasises the fact that generalisations about Chinese people who came to Australia and about the history of Chinese in different parts of Australia should not be made too freely. Among people for whom dialect, village and family groupings were considered of foremost importance, how accurate can labels such as 'Chinese' and the 'Chinese community' be? With this in mind, I will use the Chinese word *huaqiao* (華僑) to refer to those people of Chinese origin who lived in Sydney in the late nineteenth to mid-twentieth centuries. *Huaqiao*

---

* As explained in Appendix VI, there has been some research in the last 20 years that takes districts of origin into account.

literally means 'Chinese who reside away from home' and most closely corresponds to the English phrase 'overseas Chinese'. *Huaqiao* is used in order to highlight both the dangers of ignoring Henry Chan's 'ethnic and sub-ethnic groups' and to emphasise that continuing links with China for these long-term Sydney residents was crucial to their lives.[31]

Sydney

The focus on Sydney is not only due to its role as the city with the largest *huaqiao* population in Australia, but also because it was the focal point of a network of *huaqiao* businesses and communications that stretched throughout New South Wales. This network gradually shrank as the century progressed until it was restricted to inner Sydney, some Sydney suburbs and NSW regions such as the northern Tablelands.[32] Sydney is also interesting because it also had the largest Australian concentration of people from Zhongshan district, with approximately 40% of Sydney's *huaqiao* originating from there.[33]

Sources

In researching the nature of the connection between Sydney's *huaqiao* and their south China villages, the primary source was archival material from the administrative files of the Immigration Restriction Act,

1901. This material was augmented by oral evidence provided by current Sydney residents who are descendants of the *huaqiao* generation discussed in this history.* Additional material was also obtained from sources such as the late nineteenth century 'Royal Commission on Alleged Chinese Gambling', the records of the Chinese Section of Rookwood Cemetery, NSW and Commonwealth Census data, shipping records and material obtained during a field trip to Zhongshan district, south China in January 1998.

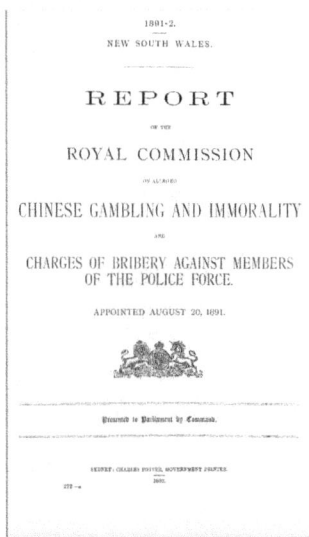

1891-2.

NEW SOUTH WALES.

R E P O R T

OF THE

ROYAL COMMISSION

ON ALLEGED

CHINESE GAMBLING AND IMMORALITY

AND

CHARGES OF BRIBERY AGAINST MEMBERS OF THE POLICE FORCE.

APPOINTED AUGUST 20, 1891.

Presented to Parliament by Command.

SYDNEY: CHARLES POTTER, GOVERNMENT PRINTER.
1892.
272 —

The Immigration Restriction Act required that non-Europeans who could prove residence in Australia before the Act's commencement (effectively February, 1902) were eligible to remain in Australia and to re-enter should they care to leave. In the course of this Act's operation over 61,668 such trips were taken between 1902 and 1946.[34] The

---

* See Appendix II for details of interviews.

administration of this Act led the Customs and Excise Offices in each State (and later the Immigration Department) to maintain files on all non-European residents in Australia every time they applied for a 'Certificate Exempting From Dictation Test' or CEDT, in order to be allowed to re-enter Australia.[35]

Due to the relative intrusiveness of this Act and its administration much evidence from its files concerning the links between Australia and the villages of origin can be gained. This material was compiled when Sydney's *huaqiao* were trying to maintain the links with their families and villages in the most tangible way. Additionally, while the Immigration Restriction Act and its 'dictation' test was primarily aimed at restricting the entry into Australia of Chinese and other non-European people, its provisions did allow for ways that people, not resident in Australia before 1901, could enter and remain in Australia. The files therefore also contain much detail on efforts to maintain and even extend the links through bringing in of wives and fellow villagers, on attempts to enter illegally, and concerning passing on the link to the next generation through sponsoring sons as assistants and students.

Perspective

The approach taken here is that of tracing the *huaqiao* as they lived and matured, that is, from arrival to marriage to old age and onto the next generation. I have taken this approach because I believe that it allows the *huaqiao's* own perspective's to be presented. This is of especial importance in a history that relies so heavily on the evidence of Immigration Restriction Act files and in a field where the Chinese have all too often been seen as 'victims' and inspirers of hostility and little else. Chapter One, 'Domiciled in the Commonwealth' discusses how it was that so many young male *huaqiao* became Sydney residents, were granted a limited right of 'domicile' by the first Federal Parliament in 1901, and why they spent many years living remitting money until they finally returned to the home village to marry. Chapter Two, 'Holiday to his own native country to see his wife and family' discusses the middle years of a Sydney *huaqiao's* life, as the now married man strove to support a growing family, to buy land and perhaps improve his family's prospects. The barriers to these aims, the paths taken by those who failed or chose to deviate from them, and the general circumstances of the wife and family in the home village are also considered. Chapter Three, 'Apart from the native born, only the old and weak are left', deals with the old age and retirement of Sydney's *huaqiao*, and the impact on the links between Sydney and south China as the next generation took over.

The title, 'Brief Sojourn in your native land'[36] is taken from a testimonial signed by a number of Gundagai residents for Mark Loong (whose picture is on the front cover) on his departure for China in 1903, after 16 years in the district. This work concerns a relationship to which the concept of a person sojourning to his native land is central. This is also a reversal of the usual idea of Chinese migrants as sojourners. The topic has been chosen because most accounts of the Chinese in Australia have revealed little about an aspect of the life of these Sydney residents that it would be difficult to deny was of great significance to most Chinese people in Australia until at least the

Mark Loong

middle of the twentieth century. It is hoped that this research will contribute to a better understanding the significance of the districts of origin, of the impact of the Immigration Restriction Act on the *huaqiao* and to how 'apparently' Australian history and south China are linked.

Testimonial signed by prominent citizens on Mark Loong's departure

CHAPTER 1
Domiciled in the Commonwealth

In 1901 the new Commonwealth Parliament passed the Immigration Restriction Act designed to make Australia a 'white' nation. This Act also granted some 30,000 people of Chinese birth the right of 'domicile' in Australia, including the right to leave and re-enter the Commonwealth. 'Domiciled in the Commonwealth'♣ examines how Sydney with its 3,500 *huaqiao* was a place where a young newly arrived 'new chum'♦ from one of the many villages of a south China district such as Zhongshan could expect to find numerous fellow villagers and speakers of his own dialect. He would also find stores and societies organised around the various south China districts of the Pearl River Delta that had the resources to help him find accommodation and work, as well as offering the important service of remitting money to maintain links with families and villages of origin until such time as they were able to make use of their

---

♣ The quote is from the Immigration Restriction Act, 1901, section 3, paragraph (n). While deleted in 1905, administrators continued to refer to 'domiciles'. See, Michael Williams, *Australia's Dictation Test: The Test it was a Crime to Fail*, Brill, 2021.

♦ 'New chum' referred to newly arrived Chinese and is possibly a loose translation of the Chinese expression, *xinke*, (新客) lit. 'new guest'. Chen Ta, op. cit., p.22, n.20, says new Chinese immigrants to Indonesia were called *Singkeh*.

'domicile' rights to return to the villages and marry. These young *huaqiao* would also find Sydney the capital of a colony which, since 1888, had severely restricted the entry and re-entry of all people of his race,[*] and where random and occasional systematic acts of discrimination and aggression against Chinese people were common.[♦]

This chapter begins with a description of the distribution by Pearl River Delta district of Sydney's *huaqiao* at the end of the nineteenth century and a discussion of the evidence for the increasing concentration of the *huaqiao* of NSW in Sydney from that time until the middle of the twentieth century. The major characteristics of the *huaqiao* on their arrival in Sydney are examined including the significance of district of origin and dialect in the organisation of support networks. Following from this, the dependence of most *huaqiao* on the support of stores and societies, particularly

---

[*] The 'Chinese Restriction and Regulation Act of 1888', defined 'Chinese' as, 'Any person of the Chinese race'. All three NSW anti-Chinese Acts (1861, 1881 and 1888) used this definition. The Commonwealth's Immigration Restriction Act, 1901 in a touching act of hypocrisy refers to no race.

[♦] See, Margaret Egerton, 'My Chinese', *The Cosmos Magazine*, September, pp.124-128, October, pp.138-141, November, pp.192-196, 1896, for a patronising but not uninformative view into the life of Sydney's *huaqiao* in the late nineteenth century, including an attack by 'larrikins' near Bondi. [For a pdf copy see: https://chinozhistory.org/index.php/no-1-my-chinese-by-margaret-egerton/] Fitzgerald, op. cit., pp.75-6 and p.94, gives examples of both.

in the maintenance of links with their home villages and families through regular remittances is discussed. Also discussed is the role of debt in the length of time spent in Sydney before a return trip to the village is made for marriage. 'Domiciled in the Commonwealth' concludes at the point the *huaqiao* are ready to use their domicile rights to maintain their links with families of their own.

Districts of Origin

The 3,500 *huaqiao* who were in Sydney at the time of the Immigration Restriction Act were all from districts from around the Pearl River Delta and these were just a small number of the Qing Empire's 1,500 districts. [37] Two witnesses to the 'Royal Commission on alleged Chinese Gambling' (referred to as Royal Commission hereafter) of 1890 provided lists of the 'communities' [districts] that were represented in Sydney around this time. Yuan Tak provided:

'Chang Sing, Toon Goon, Heong Shang, See Yip, Sam Yip, Har Kar, and Go You'.

While Robert Lee Kam gave an even more detailed list:

'There is the Chong Sing community, the Doon Goon community, the Hung Shang community, the Sun Wing community, the Sun Wiy community, the Hoy Ping community, the Ying Ping community, the Hock Sang community, the Go You community, the Go Ming community, the Sun On community, the Par Yoon community, the Sam Soon community; but there are very few individuals belonging to the last mentioned clan.'♣[38]

Allowing for variations in transcription all these communities, with the exception of the scattered 'Har Kar' (Hakka), can be identified with the districts surrounding the Pearl River Delta in southern China.♦

Sydney's *huaqiao* had ample reasons to leave their villages in Zhongshan and other Pearl River Delta districts because, throughout the nineteenth century, these districts suffered from famines, floods and civil disturbances that ranged from bandit attacks to open warfare.[39] Though it must be noted that similar problems in the other parts of China did not result in similar migration (Fujian migration to South-East Asia excepted). This was because the alleviation of such problems by emigration was acceptable to those living in the

---

♣ See Appendix I, Character Table for modern renderings of these non-standard romanisations.

♦ Compare list by Price based on 1960s Department of Immigration data, Price, op. cit., p.220, n.12, Zhongshan (40%), Gao Yao (24%), Dong Goon (20%), Sze Yap (10%), Sam Yap (3%) and non-Cantonese (2%). See also Appendix V, 'District proportions in Sydney'.

Pearl River Delta region as districts near the southern coasts of China had a tradition of overseas emigration to South-East Asia that went back to the 12th century.[40] Strong attachment to parents, along with that to the ancestral village, meant that this emigration did not occur lightly, even among families with a history of such movement. When, for example, Chang Yet, who had lived in NSW since 1898, was preparing to bring his son, Chang Gar Lock (Arthur Chang), to Australia in 1933, he first took him to the village temple, where a promise was made to the local goddess that his son would return to the village.[41]

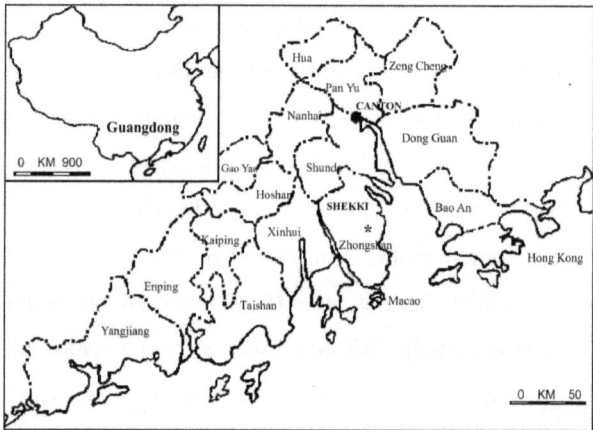

Huaqiao districts of origin, Pearl River Delta, south China.[42]

Contract labourers, generally not from the Pearl River Delta districts, were the first Chinese people to come to Australia.[43] It was the gold rushes of the 1850s, however, that brought the first significant migrations from the Pearl River Delta districts through the Port of Sydney.[44] These arrivals created in Sydney the new phenomenon of 'Chinatowns', at first in the Rocks district near the wharves and later in the Belmore Market and then Haymarket area. These 'Chinatowns' were the obvious outward signs of *huaqiao* support for each other.[45]

The passing of the gold rushes in NSW and Victoria reduced the numbers of Chinese people in the Australian colonies, but new arrivals continued and numbers began increasing again after a time. The knowledge that more money was to be earned in the Australian colonies than was ever likely to be possible in their home villages and districts, combined with the support networks that were being developed by relatives and fellow villagers who had gone before, made San Gum San/Xin Jin Shan (新金山) or the New Gold Mountain, an accessible if not always a welcoming destination for the *huaqiao*.♣ Most of the Sydney *huaqiao*

♣ This name is derived from the mid-19th century gold rush period when California was succeeded by the gold rushes of Victoria and NSW, thus becoming the Old Gold Mountain and Australia (or Victoria) the New Gold Mountain. San Francisco is still written today in Chinese as 舊金山 or Old Gold Mountain. *[The phrase "Gold Mountain" is in fact a now ubiquitous translation for the Chinese characters 金山 (gum san/jin shan) but was originally a translation choice over the more accurate if prosaic "goldfields". This is a preference that sought to make exotic what* whose rights of residence were given some recognition as 'domiciles' by the Immigration Restriction Act were in a sense the 'second' generation, those who had followed in the footsteps of the *huaqiao* of the 'gold rush'.

Demographics

By the end of the nineteenth century, Sydney found itself with a substantial Chinese population and the centre of a network of *huaqiao* connections spread throughout NSW.[46] Approximately 34% of NSW's Chinese residents lived in the then 'metropolitan' area, including most of the merchants and store owners who ran the supporting networks of stores and societies.[*] The Sydney stores of these merchants had links and shared partnerships with those in rural NSW and between them would pass remittances to the villages and imports from China such as birds' nests, smoked duck, lychees and medicine herbs.[47] These stores also provided a range of services including accommodation for *huaqiao* passing through Sydney, as the main port of NSW, to or from China.[48]

---

for Europeans was considered normal – namely, rushing to goldfields. While an attractive term that is good for titles of novels and films it should be noted that it plays a part in that "othering' of Chinese people that began in this period. Now firmly embedded in contemporary discourse it is used here and elsewhere with reservation.]

[*] See Appendix IV, Table 1 and 2.

The main occupations of Sydney's *huaqiao,* as reported by
the Chinese Gambling Commissioners were:

> ... *merchants, storekeepers, cabinet-making, market-
> gardeners, hawkers, and gamblers. It is only in cabinet-
> making and vegetable-growing, however, that they come
> into serious competition with European tradesmen.*[49]

Despite this perceived 'serious competition', the
Commissioners observed that 'in the cultivation of
vegetables the Chinese are practically masters of the
situation' and this was thought to be 'due to extreme
frugality and unremitting toil'.[50] For those *huaqiao* working
in cabinet making, country stores, and the banana trade,
however, such mastership was not to be, with *huaqiao* in all

War Sing Cabinet Makers, City of Sydney Archives

these fields experiencing racially based attacks during the late nineteenth and early twentieth centuries.[51]

Such discriminatory attacks and pressures presumably contributed to the changes in both occupations and geographic locations of the NSW *huaqiao* that occurred during the first half of the twentieth century. Analysis of the Immigration Restriction Act files reveals that NSW *huaqiao* at the beginning of the century worked in a variety of occupations and in a number of NSW locations. Both of these gradually contracted over the first 20 to 30 years of the century, with market gardening and residence in Sydney coming to predominate.[*52]

The occupations recorded in the files are more varied than those listed by the Gambling Commissioners and include market gardener, labourer, grocery storekeeper, hawker, cook, carpenter, scrub cutter, cabinet maker, tobacco farmer, miner, draper, and bookkeeper. An occupation not mentioned, but which must have been of some importance to the *huaqiao* on occasions, is that of interpreter. Long Pen was one such interpreter who claimed that he charged, 'a

---

[*] This evidence is from Immigration Restriction Act files and CEDT applications, see Appendix III for a description of the files and Appendix IV, Table 3 and 4 for statistics.

guinea a day', which compared well to a market gardeners' £1 per week.[*][53]

Information from CEDT applications indicates a wide range of NSW locations initially but, in the later applications, it is Sydney and its suburbs that are listed more often. Census data confirms this evidence of chan ging settlement patterns. Sydney in 1901 had 34% of the NSW *huaqiao* population. By 1921 this had risen to around 40% and to over 50% by 1933. As a proportion of the Australian *huaqiao* population, Sydney also rose (as did NSW), from 11.8% in 1901 to 17.4% by 1933.[54] The trend is even more pronounced by 1947 when it is influenced by refugees who arrived mostly in Sydney.

Certificate Exempting From Dictation Test.
The records of applications over half a century provide a wealth of statistics.[55]

[*] A guinea being £1 and 1 shilling.

Regardless of occupation or where they lived, the most obvious feature of the *huaqiao* as a whole and one often commented on was that they were almost entirely men.[56] Less obvious perhaps was that they were 'nearly all farmers and labourers' who had arrived in Sydney and other Australian ports as young men or even boys.[57] The evidence of the CEDT applications is that *huaqiao* of the 'domicile' generation were aged on average between 16 and 25 years when they left their villages.*

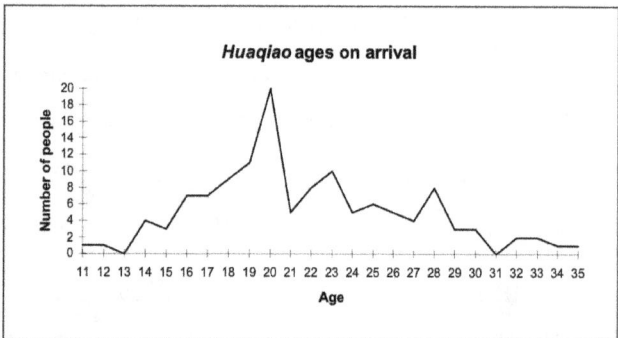

Huaqiao ages on arrival

Chart 1: An 11 year old boy and a 35 year old man represent the extremes of the files sampled.[58]

The attitude of traditional Chinese culture to parents and related ideas about the function of marriage helps to explain why *huaqiao* emigration before the twentieth century was

---

* See Appendix IV, Tables 1 and 2.

predominantly male. It was the view that a woman's role was not only to marry, but that as a wife, her role was to support her husband's parents more than it was to take care of that husband.♣[59] Arthur Chang illustrates an aspect of these attitudes when he reports attending a proxy marriage in his village in the 1920s where the groom was represented by a rooster. The son in this case was already married and living in Australia but his mother had insisted on a second wife to look after her in China.[60]

District Societies & Stores

On arrival in Sydney, these young men found associations and stores to assist them in various ways. Unlike Chinese cities, whose workers were organised around occupational guilds, the *huaqiao* in the cities of the Chinese diaspora, such as Sydney, relied on regional associations for social and political organisation.[61] These *tongxiang* (同鄉), or 'same place' societies, provided some of the support necessary for the *huaqiao* to survive and prosper in a city dominated by people of another culture. These societies, as the Chinese Gambling Commissioners described them, were 'benevolent institutions, formed on the basis of 'cousinship', and displaying their charity in the transport

---

♣ See Appendix VI for research in the last 20 years focused on women.

of old men and the bones of their deceased countrymen to China'.[62] The societies raised their money from members subscriptions with, according to Yuen Tak of the Koon Yee Tong, nobody being, 'allowed to pay less than £1, but many of the merchants paid as much as £5, £10, and £50'.[63] They also, according to a researcher of regional organisations in Hong Kong, played a significant role in 'keeping *huaqiao* focused on their obligations to their families in the village'.[64] This last was a factor of some importance, given the length of time many *huaqiao* were separated from their families.

The Loong Yee Tong continues to operate in
Dixon Street, Sydney.

These societies were run by the same merchants who owned the stores the average *huaqiao* used for support and assistance.[65] This was part of a paternalism which, Ah Way explained to the Commissioners, was the basis of the role his grandfather, Way Kee, played in the Koon Yee Tong of the Doon Goon district people. It was not a question of his seeking election but, 'on account of seeing that my grandfather was in such a larger way of business, and was trusted, these men would take their money to him to keep for them'. The men he was referring to were those principally in 'the gardening or hawking line'.[66] A man in Way Kee's position was obliged to help others of his community. As Ah Way again explained, 'if my grandfather did not go and bail them [Chinese arrested for gambling] out, being a leading man, it would not look well.'[67]

A prominent characteristic of people from the Pearl River Delta districts was their strong identification by district and dialect, and these affiliations were a significant factor in determining the profile of the societies and network of stores formed by the *huaqiao* in Sydney and elsewhere.[68] This was the 'cousinship' the Chinese Gambling Commissioners referred to as the basis of the societies they were investigating. Most Sydney *huaqiao* spoke the Yue language (Cantonese), but with variations that made the members of the different districts readily distinguishable.

Some groups, such as the Hakka (客家) and people from the Long Dou (隆都) area within Zhongshan, spoke a non-Yue language that was unintelligible to the majority of Cantonese speakers.[69] Up to half of the Zhongshan people of Sydney were reported to be from this single Long Dou area and the people of this district felt an affinity with each other that extended beyond that of village and family.[70]

Generally, each district had its own society, though some had more than one and some combined to form a single society, such as the Dong Guan and Zeng Cheng people did to form the Loong Yee Tong.[71] Why some districts had more than one society, whether this was because of different functions or because of differing groups within a district, is unclear. The Commissioners needed to have the 'exclusiveness' of the societies explained to them on a number of occasions, such as when Way Shong stated that, 'Moy Ping is not of my community – he would not subscribe', and when Sam Tin needed to explain that he was denying membership of the Loong Yee Tong, not because it was a gambling society but rather 'as I do not belong to that part of the country they would not let me in it'.[72]

Apart from the district societies, the young *huaqiao* were assisted by stores also organised by district and patronised almost exclusively by customers of that district. As San Tin reported of his Lodging House, 'only friends and countrymen [district] stop there'.[73] People without a district related store of their own could use the services of other stores, but for sending remittances and other assistance relative to their own villages, they were not of great use.[74] The role of these stores in linking Sydney's *huaqiao* to the villages of their districts reached such a level that most things could be organised through them. The main Zhongshan firms, Wing On & Co., Onyik Lee & Co. and the Kwong War Chong, paid fares, purchased tickets, arranged Immigration Restriction Act related paper work, provided accommodation and even lent money for the first remittance home, including a letter written by the firm's scribe if necessary. This last was referred to as 'Returning Gold' (回金) and signalled safe arrival.[75]

These Sydney based stores were able to provide services that reached back to the villages because they were part of a network of stores related by ownership and/or common partners in Hong Kong and the home districts.[76] The 'General Merchants' firm of Sun Sam Choy, for example, had 25 partners, only five of whom were in Sydney itself, nine were in Newcastle (where there was perhaps a branch store), one in Glenn Innes, eight in Hong Kong and a further two in Canton.[77] In the Zhongshan district capital, Shekki,

(石岐, Shiqi), the Kwong War Fong (廣和丰) was the branch firm of the Kwong War Chong (廣和豐) of Sydney.[78] Kwong War Chong & Co. was typical of many *huaqiao* businesses in being founded by numerous partners, in this case seven, all holding equal shares. All the partners, except one, arrived in Sydney before 1902 and all, except the Australian-born sons of one of the partners, had returned to China by the 1930s.[79]

Philip Lee Chun
Last remaining partner of the Kwong War Chong

The dependence of the *huaqiao* on stores such as the Kwong War Chong was high. Life in Sydney for the average *huaqiao* meant living in a land dominated by people whose culture and habits they considered inferior, whose language they did not speak or did not speak well, and who were not only prejudiced against Chinese as a race but had the power to act upon that prejudice.[80] Circumstances such as these, combined with the strong district orientation and local self-support character of the *huaqiao's* cultural background, made a high level of group self-sufficiency among Sydney's *huaqiao* natural.[81]

One of the manners of this co-operation and support was noted in the common perception and complaint against Chinese people by Europeans around the turn of the century that they worked for less and so undercut other workers.[82] A police report in 1916 described the practical basis of this in that 'the keeper of every cabinetmaker's shop, produce, fruit and grocery store, employ large numbers of chinese [sic] (aliens) who are paid a weekly wage, and are provided with accommodation for their services'.[83] These wages were significantly lower than the average, with cabinet makers in 1899 recorded as being paid an average wage of £2/8/-, while Chinese cabinet makers received £1/11/6. Similarly, cooks were recorded as averaging £2 per week, while Chinese cooks earned only £1/2/-.[84]

33

Returning home

While most *huaqiao* were working at these occupations they also presumably wished to see again the families they had left at such a young age and which they may have been helping to support. Figures derived from the CEDT records suggest that while most *huaqiao* made such a trip, they waited a considerable length of time before they did so. Sydney's share of the total NSW *huaqiao* population of 10,000 in 1901 was only about 3,500, yet from 1902 to 1959 a total of 27,654 people identified as 'Chinese' passed through Sydney on CEDTs. With many multiple journeys, it is difficult to determine how many *huaqiao* actually returned to the home village, or at least to China, and how many did not. As some *huaqiao* made only one or two trips, many four or five and some as many as ten, a simple calculation is not possible short of reviewing every file. If four to five trips per person is taken as an average, it can perhaps be stated that more than 6,000 individual *huaqiao* living in NSW, out of an initial population in 1901 of 10,000, made at least one China trip.*[85] Of those that did make such a trip, some spent from 10 to 20, and in many cases, 30 to 40 years, working, remitting and living a 'bachelor' life in Australia before seeing their families and villages again.

---

* See Appendix IV, Table 9.

34

Chart 2: One *huaqiao* did not return for 49 years. Many of course did not return at all. See Appendix IV, Table 6.

The major reason such lengthy periods were spent working alone in a foreign land would appear to be that for cash-poor peasants the cost of a passage to Sydney was too great. 'Some said that they did not even have the half dollar to pay the boat fare from the mainland to Hong Kong.'[86] In order for *huaqiao* to get to Sydney at all, it was often necessary to become indebted to those, such as an agent operating through Hong Kong or a relative who had sufficient money after his own sojourn, who would pay for their passage.[87]

This method of migration was known as the 'credit-ticket' system and required the young *huaqiao* to repay the debt incurred in buying his passage before anything else. 'For

35

each tael I must repay two taels.'[88] Referring to the cabinet-making industry the Chinese Gambling Commissioners described the system as 'indentures under which new arrivals were compelled to work for certain periods at excessively low rates'. [89] The Commissioners also had described to them how a Dr On Lee brought in 30 immigrants, paid the £100 poll tax on them and then deducted this from their wages.* The agreement was that they would work in his gardens for five years. [90] After paying such debts, the *huaqiao* were free to save to purchase a share in a market garden or other business, and remit what they could to their parents in the village. It was only when these parents announced they had saved sufficient to arrange a suitable marriage, or if this became increasingly unlikely, saved sufficient himself, could the *huaqiao* finally return to begin to raise a family of his own.[91]

For the *huaqiao*, it was essential that the family in the village was supported and even a small amount of money in Sydney went a long way in a south China village. Despite their lower wages, the lower living costs due to the provision of board and lodging and having no family to support in Sydney meant that it was possible to remit money to the

---

* A £100 poll tax was introduced under the 'Chinese Restriction and Regulation Act of 1888'. It was £10 when first introduced in 1881.

village. According to the rough estimate of the Chinese Gold Commissioners, based on what they were told by Quain Young, it cost 'four times as much to feed a man here', while wages were, '20 times as great'.[92] It was in their assistance with this purpose that the stores played a crucial role in the life of Sydney's *huaqiao*. Over time a reliable system developed for remitting money through those stores with branches or connections in Hong Kong, and from there back to the districts and villages. How this system of store-based remittances came about is described by Way Kee when he explained to the Commissioners that 'he sent home in the same box [as his £10,000] some money from Chinamen here who wished to send to their parents or friends in China'.[93] Such remittances were known as 'se ling dan' (司令單) or sterling because English pounds were used as the currency of exchange due to their stability.[94]

The Kwong War Chong was the Zhongshan store most used by market gardeners from that district. It was established in 1883 in Campbell St by several partners, including Philip Lee Chun who had come to Australia in 1874. The store moved to 84 Dixon St in 1910, where it operated as a general store and trading company until 1987.* The store stocked

---

* The building was belatedly recognised as of State Heritage in 2024 but not in time to save it from destructive redevelopment.

everything the *huaqiao* might need, especially the type of goods they might want to take back with them to the village, such as boiled lollies, Arnott's biscuits (Scotch Fingers and Arrowroots, rather than creams), and umbrellas. [95] The Kwong War Chong was also a major remittance centre for Zhongshan *huaqiao*, though stores such as Wing On & Co. also remitted.[96]

Remittances

Nineteenth century remittances may have been taken in the form of gold, as Way Kee described, and during World War One it was the opinion of the Comptroller-General of Trade & Customs, when gold exports were limited to £50 per person, that 'particular note of them [Chinese passengers] should be taken'.[97] By the 1930s, bank drafts were more common and in this case a store collected the individual remittances from its customers and a standard letter was written to the family, usually by the store's clerk as 'they were not much letter writers', to accompany the payment.[98] The store charged a small commission on each remittance and consolidated all the monies into a single draft drawn on the English, Scottish and Australian Bank in pounds sterling. The draft was then sent to the Hong Kong branch of the Kwong War Chong, where it was converted to Hong Kong dollars and then into Chinese dollars for the money to be sent to Shekki. The store's branch in Shekki then distributed the money to the families, either by their collecting it or it being delivered to the village by the firm's clerks. A receipt, which included a letter back to the *huaqiao* in Sydney, would be signed and returned to the shop in Dixon St, where it was set up on a rack in the front window for people to collect.[99]

This remittance system was not based on contractual or legally enforceable arrangements and such informal procedures had their risks. Once a remittance customer complained that his family had not gotten their money and accused Philip Lee Chun, Manager of the Kwong War Chong, of stealing the remittance. Philip Lee Chun was sitting outside his shop in Dixon St one evening, 'taking the air' when, according to his son Norman Lee, he was suddenly struck on the head by a piece of 'two by four'. The man later apologised when his family sent word that they had received the money.[100]

The amount of money remitted naturally varied with the earnings of the individual. In 1891, Chow Kum, a carpenter and furniture maker, stated that he sent £20 per year to his wife.[101] For the family of Lee Man Dick, a Rockdale storekeeper and market garden owner, it was considered enough for his family in China to live on.[102] While for the family of Chang Yet, a carpenter, the income from the land of his grandmother was also necessary to make the family comfortable.[103] John Louie Hoon's family, on the other hand, was not able to buy any land with his remittances earned as a market gardener.[104] While Joe Wah Gow, a Wollongong store owner, was able to retire on 600 *mu*, compared to Chang Yet's 50 *mu* of rice land.[105]

Joe Wah Gow and his family

Parents & Wives

Initially remittances were sent to a *huaqiao's* parents because, while district and dialect was significant to the *huaqiao* in Sydney, it was fidelity to family and especially to parents that provided the most important attachment to the home village. The significance of parents in traditional Chinese culture is illustrated in the explanation the manager of Onyik & Lee Co. gave in 1902, to the NSW Collector of Customs as to why Tommy Way, among others, left Sydney without the Certificate authorising their return. Tommy Way, 'like many Chinese were forced to go to their native country to visit their parents'. [106] Numerous written references supplied by *huaqiao* with their applications for Certificates Exempting from Dictation Test (CEDT) throughout the early part of the twentieth century, refer to visiting parents as the reason for the trip.[107]

References only later in a *huaqiao's* life refer to wife and family rather than parents. Nevertheless, that it was usually after the first trip back to the home village that most Sydney *huaqiao* married can be surmised from the CEDT applications. Questions about a person's family appeared from 1902 to 1905, then were removed and did not reappear on CEDT applications again until 1930. A comparison of the answers to these questions, including files that cover both these periods, reveals that 75% of *huaqiao* reported

41

that they had married after their first sojourn to the village (see Appendix IV, Table 7).[108] Or to put it another way, they made their first trip back when they were ready to marry.

The decision of so many *huaqiao* to marry in the village was not only the result of custom and parental wish but also because of limited choice. The great imbalance between the sexes, whether created by Chinese cultural norms or European legal restrictions, imposed a basic restriction on the choices available to the *huaqiao*. The Commonwealth Census of 1911 records 801 Chinese out of a total male population of 21,032, living with wives in Australia and a further 6,714 were recorded to have wives in China. The places of birth of the Australian based wives were recorded as, 'China born' - 181, 'England' - 63, 'Scot' - 15, 'Ireland' – 22 and 'Australia born' – 485. This last group are assumed to be 'Chinese or mixed', though on what basis is unclear.[109]

For the 13,000 in Australia and proportionally 1,900 Sydney *huaqiao* who were unmarried, the choice, for those who hoped to do so, was to wait until they returned to the village or to marry in Australia. Those marrying in China could leave the wife in the village or attempt to bring her to Australia. Those marrying in Australia could seek to marry one of the few Chinese or Chinese descended women in Australia, or they could marry a non-Chinese woman.♣[110]

There is evidence that each of these alternatives had their takers but the proportion of *huaqiao* that may have taken each path is difficult to determine.♦ The majority of *huaqiao* had neither the status nor the money necessary to bring their wives to Australia, or were held to the traditional role of the wife as support for their own parents. For them, as the large number of wives in China show, the choice was limited to a village marriage and to maintaining that wife and the resulting family in the village.[111]

The option to bring a wife to Australia was actually recognised by the 1901 Immigration Restriction Act though restricted this in practice to 'merchants' wives. However, after 1903 this option was reduced to a temporary entry only with no particular preference for 'merchants' as such.♥[112]

♣ Joe Wah Gow even managed to marry an Australian born Chinese girl that he met in China, interview with Victor Gow, 30 October 1997 (3).

♦ See Appendix VI for more recent research on women in the last 20 years.

♥ Like all the Immigration Restriction Act there is no mention of Chinese men or their wives as such. Paragraph (m) in full reads that entry to Australia is allowed by:

(m) a wife accompanying her husband if he is not a prohibited immigrant, and all children apparently under the age of eighteen years accompanying their father or mother if the

This proclamation is often misinterpreted as a ban on women but there was never such a ban and this merely eliminates a slight encouragement that existed briefly.

Yee See was one of the few women who took advantage of this brief encouragement. The wife of Philip Lee Chun she arrived in Sydney in 1903 aged 19 and remained there for the rest of her life even after her husband had returned to China to die in 1931. Despite her bound feet her son William Lee reported he often took her to the theatre.

father or mother is not a prohibited immigrant; but so that the exceptions in this paragraph shall not apply if suspended by proclamation; and such suspension may be of general application or limited to any cases or class of cases.

These legalities acted more to reinforce already existing patterns rather than impose any great change. The Chinese Gambling Commissioners were told that 'the majority of them who come here are too poor to pay the passage money for their wives', and even Way Kee, a rich merchant, waited 22 years before bringing his wife to Sydney.[113] Being well established was a significant factor, as Chow Kum explained, 'now that my business is established I would [bring his wife out] ... but at the time the poll tax was low I could not afford to bring her out'.[114]

Those *huaqiao* most independent of traditional culture were also those given the most leeway by the restrictive legislation. Thus when after 1903 wives could enter Australia only temporarily, extensions were often sought to try and convert a temporary stay into a permanent one.[115] This was done in the case of Chang Wai Sheu Sing whose wife, Chun Sue Moy, entered Sydney on a temporary Certificate of Exemption in February 1927.✲ Through numerous extensions and the judicious building up of a trading firm, the couple were able to remain long enough in Sydney to be among the first China born people to take up

---

✲ A 'Certificate of Exemption' should not be confused with a 'Certificate Exempting from Dictation Test' or CEDT which was given to pre-1901 domiciles only. See Appendix III, C.

the right of Australian Citizenship when this was finally granted to Chinese people in 1958.[116]

Those *huaqiao* that did marry in Australia, whether to Chinese, non-Chinese or women of mixed parentage, did not have the same incentive to return to the village as those with wives there. A factor that may have contributed to the choice to marry in Australia and/or not to return was that a *huaqiao's* parents may have already died or contact with them lost. Sun War Hop insisted he would 'go home to see my old father and mother', even though with a wife and business in Sydney he would not, as the Commissioners put it, 'give up this country'.[117] Louie Gay, a well-to-do market gardener, who married Ada, an Australian born Chinese of mixed parentage, never returned to the village despite owning land there, assisting his brothers to come to Australia and even sending one of his sons to live there for three years.[118] Philip Lee Chun, the manager of the Kwong War Chong, once he brought his wife Yee See to Sydney in 1903, did not return to China again until, in his 70s, he travelled to Hong Kong in 1931, where he died and from where his body was transported back to his village by junk.[119]

Despite their greater chances of bringing a wife from China, merchants and storekeepers were also more likely to marry the few Chinese or part-Chinese women who were in Australia. While poorer *huaqiao* were more likely to marry, or at least live, with non-Chinese women. Perhaps because they were 'so lonely they married Australian girls', as one explanation has it.[120] The 'intermarriage' option was one that was disagreeable to both Chinese and European cultures throughout the period though as, the 1911 census figures indicate, many did take this option.[121]

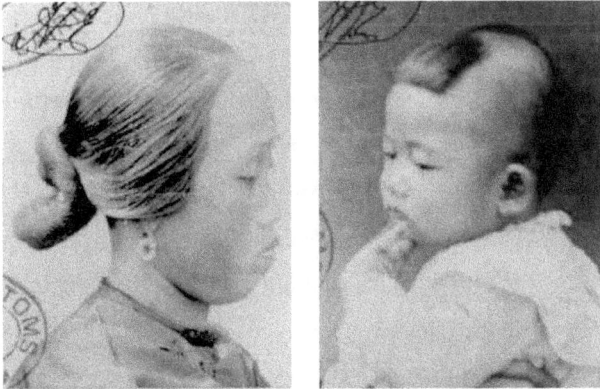

Leong Ah Wan was one of the relatively few wives resident in Australia. In 1908 she went with her daughter Nellie on a trip to China.

Two or more wives were also possible given the Chinese tradition of wives and concubines.[122] Just how common this practice may have been is impossible to say. The Chinese Gambling Commissioners were told that 'Yuan Tak has two Chinese wives and children living on the rocks [sic] in great style.'[123] While Way Shong explained that he has one wife in China and one here because, 'the old wife sent this one out, so that I might have children. That is the usual custom in China'.[124] Young Sow reported to Immigration officials in 1963 that he had three wives, one in Sydney and two in Hong Kong, a revelation noted without comment by the officials.[125] While in 1956, William Bun applied for the admission into Australia of his wife in China soon after his Australian born wife had died.[126]

A final 'choice' that an indeterminate number of *huaqiao* made was to neither marry nor return. Many village members who left for Australia simply 'disappeared' as far as their village was concerned. Sometimes family in the village might make an effort to contact them but this could easily be ignored. A rough estimate of the proportion that might fall into this category was four to five percent of the *huaqiao* population.[127] There could be many reasons why this path was taken. When Chow Kum, for example, was asked why the old don't go back to China he replied, 'Because they have no money. As a general rule their money has all gone in opium-smoking and gambling, and they have become too old to do anything to make any more.' Chow Kum applied the same thinking to himself, 'Of course if I could not make enough money I should have to remain here'.[128] To return without money would be an admission of failure and some chose to cut all ties to the family and village rather than do so.[129] For those who could not face cutting the links with their family, there was no choice other than to keep working, to repay their debts, to remit money and to await the right time to marry.

Conclusion

Thus far a pattern of living for the majority of *huaqiao* in Sydney has been identified that involved frugal living, dependence and co-operation on district stores and societies, regular remittance of savings, a long initial period in Australia, and the need to return to the village to marry. The limited recognition of rights of residence extended by the Immigration Restriction Act in 1901, in conjunction with support networks within the district communities, saw the *huaqiao* of Sydney in a reasonable position to return to their villages. Once, that is, hard work and thrift had enabled them to gradually save towards the point at which they could return home and marry. The following chapter will discuss how the *huaqiao* continued to rely on these networks as they worked and remitted money to support a wife and growing family.

CHAPTER 2

Holiday to his own native country to see his wife and family

Once married, free of debt and perhaps with a share in a market garden, the *huaqiao* were in a position to greatly increase their links with the home village. The most obvious way to do this was to visit the village, to take a 'holiday to his own native country to see his wife and family',[130] as one non-Chinese individual perhaps rather naively put it.

Increased trips of the *huaqiao* to visit their growing families, despite the restrictions imposed by the Immigration Restriction Act, is a major feature of their middle years. The family and villages of the *huaqiao* are influenced by these visits. While China's deteriorating political and social conditions, ranging from the threat of attacks by bandits to both civil and international war, also have their effect. Efforts by the *huaqiao* of Sydney to bring more people into Australia, including illegally, are part of this developing relationship, as is a sharp decline in overall numbers.♣

The effect of the discriminatory laws in re-enforcing some existing patterns and slowing change is seen again in the

---

♣ For more on smuggling as an aspect of the links see Michael Williams, "Stopping them Using Our Boats", *Australian Economic History Review*, 61(1), pp.64–79, 2020.

continued dependency of the *huaqiao* on the stores and the merchants who ran them.

We begin by discussing the evidence for the increased frequency of trips and of the various barriers to these trips raised by the administration of the Immigration Restriction Act. These barriers are seen to range from minor bureaucratic procedures to those necessitating dependence upon the district stores and possibly, to those that effectively break the links with China for some *huaqiao*. The 'illegal' element in the links between Sydney and the villages is also examined. That side of the relationship represented by the 'wife and family' in the 'native country' is considered, including the purposes that the remittances are put to, the role of the wife in the family and the impact of the *huaqiao* on the village through donations. The background of social and political disruption is illustrated and the hazards for *huaqiao* on 'holiday', including bandits, are seen. Finally, alternatives that some *huaqiao* took, such as ceasing to travel or moving the family to Hong Kong are discussed.

The average time many *huaqiao* spent in Sydney before their first trip home to the village was 10 to 20 years.[*] Once this initial trip back was made, however, subsequent trips

---

[*] See Chapter 1, Chart 2, above.

became more frequent, roughly every two to three years and lasting an average of 12 to 18 months. Occasionally, a stay in China of 7 to 10 years occurred but the frequency and length of the sojourns was generally uniform.[131] One reason for the narrow range of periods spent in China was probably the fact that to stay more than 36 months required an extension to the CEDT.

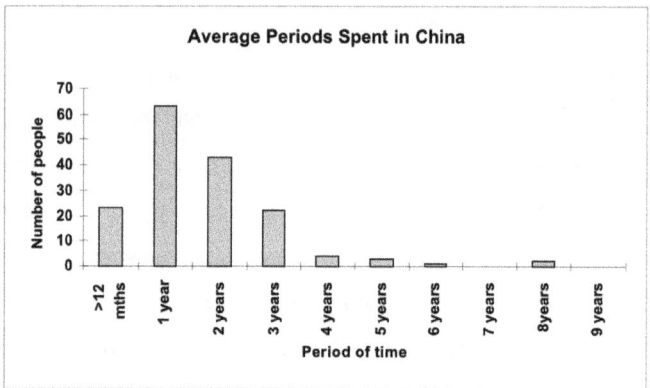

Chart 3: Times spent in the villages generally kept within that laid down by the CEDTs.*

In the 1930s, Billy Gay, whose father owned a large market garden at Granville on the then western edge of Sydney, knew many *huaqiao* who would, 'go back for 12 months' whenever they had saved £100.[132] Lee Man Dick was typical of a well-to-do *huaqiao* in his sojourning. He was 11

_____

* See Appendix IV, Table 9.

years in Australia before his first trip back to his 'native land' in 1912. Thereafter he made 10 trips to his village of Gam Wan/Jin Huan (金環), before his retirement trip in 1956, aged 75. Lee Man Dick usually stayed in the village between one and a half to two and a half years, and for slightly longer periods in his Rockdale fruit and vegetable shop.[133]

Lee Man Dick, a well-to-do *huaqiao* and his two wives. The wives remained in the village to look after the children and the land.[134]

Huaqiao such as Lee Man Dick were required to comply with the various restrictions of the Immigration Restriction Act in order to maintain links with their home villages. The consequences of these restrictions ranged from maintaining *huaqiao* dependence upon their district stores to possibly preventing links continuing for those denied CEDTs before leaving or denied re-entry on their attempt to return to Australia.

The Immigration Restriction Act, as with most laws and regulations, required people to adapt or appear to adapt, their behaviour.* The earliest example of such adaptations occurred when those administering the legislation began by interpreting the 'domicile' requirement as 'intention to establish a permanent home' rather than evidence of pre-1901 domicile, leading as a result to a number of early refusals to grant Certificates of Domicile.[135] William Wong Gip was refused a certificate in June 1902 because he 'has a wife and son in China and therefore does not come within

the lines laid down to qualify him for a Certificate of Domicile'.♦ [136] This interpretation quickly became known among the *huaqiao* and by May 1902 'it was understood that permits would not be granted to Chinese gardeners'.[137]

William's Christianity did not help him.

---

* For a complete history of the administration of the Dictation Test see, Michael Williams, *Australia's Dictation Test: The Test it was a Crime to Fail*, Brill, 2021.

♦ See Appendix III, C for a summary of the basic CEDT procedures.

However, this interpretation on the part of officials and its even more extreme interpretation among *huaqiao* gardeners themselves, seems to have rapidly altered. In November 1902, a Department of External Affairs minute referred to 5 years residence and a settled business as a 'general rule'.[138] Complaints by the shipping companies at the loss of passengers and protests by the *huaqiao* themselves may have influenced this decision.[139] Whatever the reason, by February 1903, War Sing, a cook with substantial liquid assets but no property, was granted a certificate even before his efforts to purchase property had been made known to the Collector of Customs through his solicitor.[140]

Within a few years of the Act's commencement this interpretation had relaxed to the extent that Tommy Way, who had no CEDT, could be granted 'admission on being identified'. [141] Ah Way, a Fairfield market gardener, was also permitted to return without a Certificate of Domicile after an absence of eight years when Joe Que wrote on his behalf to explain that 'he was unfortunately

Tommy was a cook with substantial savings

55

unaware how to obtain the permit to allow him to return'.[142] A relatively relaxed attitude to such matters was essential if the links with the home villages were to be maintained and the *huaqiao* were not to be forced to choose between the income they could earn and their families in China.♣[143]

Falling numbers

The small amount of leeway allowed by the administrators of the Act was contingent, as far as 'White Australia' was concerned, upon the total Chinese population of Australia falling. The *status quo,* which included *huaqiao* travelling, created by the Act and its administrators was dependent on such a fall being the case. In 1908, the Act's administrators, concerned to know whether Sydney's Chinese population was falling, undertook a 'Check on importation of Chinese Goods'. It was reported that, 'so far at any rate as this test may be relied upon, ... the Chinese population of this State is certainly not on the increase'.♦[144] Similarly, the 1925

♣ Not that the administrators of the Immigration Restriction Act did not continue to be zealous in their work. When a ship's crewman suffered a mental illness and was placed in Callen Park Hospital it was considered, 'desirable to issue a Certificate of Exemption, which may be renewed from time to time, so that in the event of the patient recovering he may be required to leave the Commonwealth'.

♦ In 1962, a check of statistics was again done by the administrators of immigration at that time to ensure that modifications in policy had not resulted in a major change in Chinese numbers. One difference between the check of 1908

Commonwealth Year Book contained a special section on the 'Chinese in Australia' which reported with satisfaction that, 'as only 2,026 of the 17,157 Chinese recorded in 1921 were born in this country, the decrease is likely to continue'.[145]

While the bulk of *huaqiao* who wished were apparently able to do so, the opportunity to visit their home village, or anywhere else, could be refused individuals on the basis of their 'character'. To assist in making this judgement amendments to the Act in 1905 saw the 'Certificate of Domicile' replaced with the 'Certificate Exempting From Dictation Test' (CEDT), which required applicants to supply at least two written references.[146] Kee Sun, for example, was refused a certificate because his Pitt St Tobacconist Shop was a well-known gambling establishment.[147] While She Jin was also refused on the 'grounds of bad character and misstatements as to how he had been employed', he was eventually granted a certificate, however, 'in view of further representations'.*[148]

It was presumably the assumption that *huaqiao* with such undesirable characters would wish to leave Australia

---

and that of 1962 was that the later file was marked 'Secret (To be passed by Hand)'.

* By Senator Bakhap

eventually and should not be able to return. It was just as likely, perhaps, that settlement in Australia was encouraged by weakening the links *huaqiao* such as Kee Sun or She Jin had with their home districts.

The link could be more directly broken by a *huaqiao* being refused entry on return to Sydney. Harry Chun Fook, known as a 'K.M.T. basher',♦ [149] was refused re-entry on the suspicion that he

Tasmanian Senator Bakhap, was a Chinese speaker and the adopted son of a Chinese born man. Image NLA.

had originally entered illegally. When he was allowed to enter, he not only faced prosecution as a 'prohibited migrant' but the burden of proof lay with him to demonstrate that he was not one. The charges were dropped partly because the 'fact that the man has a white wife and a child here would create difficulties in the way of deporting

---

♦ 'He has assaulted by means of a knuckle duster, other Chinese who held opposite political views to those of the Kuo Ming Tang.'

him...' [150] Chong Dye also had a non-Chinese wife in Australia when he was refused both re-entry and permission to land. The reason for the refusal was coyly explained to the Rev T. O. Todd, who had written a letter of support, to be 'owing to the unsatisfactory nature' of his calling.[151]

Entry denied

People could also be refused re-entry and their chances of earning money to support their families lost on such grounds as in Yet Hing's case, that his photo did not look like him, or Yook Fong's, when all references by Chinese people as to his identity were refused. [152] 'Identification' was the key, as William Ah Ping

Yet Hing

discovered when doubt was expressed about his being the age shown on his NSW Birth Certificate. As an experiment William Ah Ping found himself being X-rayed to determine his age by the 'condition of ossification' of his bones. The experiment cost NSW Customs £3/3/0 and was not attempted again.[153]

Identification was even more difficult when the only picture available was of a *huaqiao* as a baby. In the case of 18 year old

Norman Charles Aubrey Mar Young

Norman Charles Aubrey Mar Young, it took the combined statutory declarations of his father, several friends and finally his grandmother, who was European, before he was allowed to enter free of a £100 bond.[154]

A further restriction to a *huaqiao's* 'holiday' was the limited validity of the CEDT. While the 36 month limit to the CEDT was more generous than the nine months granted under NSW's 1881 Act, the limitation still caused difficulties when a sojourn was prolonged by the illness or death of parents or other circumstances.[155] Ah Yaut or Jow Kue* needed to apply for re-entry into Australia in 1907 after having been away five years. Ah Yaut did what many thousands of *huaqiao* did subsequently, he wrote to a store in Sydney, in this case Ben Hing & Co., and requested the manager to negotiate with NSW Customs on his behalf.[156] A request was made for further evidence and Ah Yaut wrote

---

* See Appendix I regarding Chinese names.

explaining how his father, then mother became ill, then how his father died and finally his mother. Ah Yaut was given a letter, via Ben Hing & Co., to enable him to purchase his steamer ticket in Hong Kong and then to land in Sydney, where he would be identified and a CEDT extension granted retrospectively. [157] The issue of such letters and retrospective CEDT's became standard practice by the 1920s, while requests for further evidence were dispensed with.

Ah Yaut obtained one of the first Certificates of Domicile issued in 1903 in Sydney. These were replaced around 1907 with CEDTs.[158]

The Hidden

Such administrative procedures seemingly did no more than impose on people the necessity for much letter writing, waiting and a re-enforced dependence upon their district stores. It is not known, however, how many *huaqiao* were discouraged from applying at all, nor what anxiety or hardship was caused. Also, since the evidence about extensions is from the files of those who continued to travel between Australia and China, it must underestimate the numbers of those who were denied extensions, while making it seem that all requests for extensions were granted. Without a record of rejections, for which therefore no file was created, it is impossible to estimate how many people were denied re-entry.

Defiance

While some people may have been discouraged by the Act's requirements, others were prepared to defy it entirely. Officials were more concerned with this standpoint and it was their belief that not only had people entered Australia illegally but that they would try to pass themselves off as pre-1901 'domiciles', even to the extent of attempting a return visit to China. Officials were warned that, 'Particular care is desirable when comparatively young looking Chinese (who may claim to be over 40, but look younger) state that they have been in Australia since prior to December, 1901 and have not since been absent.'[159]

When Ah Moy and Yum Leong applied to make their first trips back to China after 31 and 46 years respectively in Australia, officials suspected that they had entered illegally after 1901 and were posing as 'domiciles'.[160] Whatever the reasons that made each wish to go to China after such a long period, they were urgent enough that both left without CEDTs. Both, however, returned and were able to convince officials that they were in fact pre-1901 'domiciles' and allowed to re-enter. Whether or not illegal entrants would have dared to take such risks is difficult to say, but that officials believed some *huaqiao* might try is demonstrated by their behaviour in these cases.

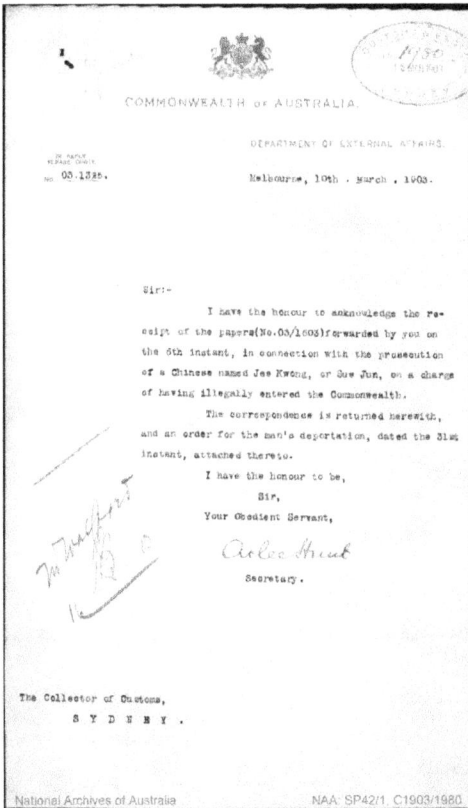

Jee Kwong's deportation

The purchase of false Naturalisations and CEDTs was one of many illegal methods used to enter Australia as, for example, when Ah Shing confessed to paying £25 in Hong Kong to purchase NSW Naturalisation papers.[161] Corrupt officials supplying false identification as a returned domicile was another method.[162] More common, however, were 'deserters' as crew leaving a ship were called, such as Jee Kwong, who left his ship and was caught and deported in 1903, or Lois Poy who received 8 weeks gaol for desertion plus one week as an illegal immigrant before being deported in 1911. [163] Chan Chee was perhaps too determined. He was caught and returned to his ship from which he, 'jumped overboard, the *St. Albans* being then about 1 mile from Sydney Heads, and it is believed was drowned'.[164]

The method that seems to have added to Sydney's *huaqiao* population more than any other was the smuggling of people on board ships.[165] These were usually part of an organised effort that included crew members and the planning of people in both Hong Kong and Sydney. The prospective *huaqiao* were concealed in such places as coal bunkers and water tanks, and as these last were inside the 'Chinese passengers quarters', returning *huaqiao* presumably knew all about this alternative method of emigration. [166] They were not very comfortable alternatives, with some stowaways being reported, 'too weak to leave' the ship and others found dead in their suffocating hiding places.[167]

In 1908, the Revenue Detective Inspector submitted to the Acting Collector of Customs, NSW, a detailed report, 'relative to the evasion of the Act by the connivance of the crews of vessels' concerning, 'some of the methods adopted in the past'. The report explains the rise in numbers of people engaged in 'the business' as due to past success, that the £80 cost was divided between the 'shipper' in Hong Kong and the 'assistant' in Australia, and how the crews of the 'E.&A. line'* were the worst and had at one time built a space in the 'Melbourne cargo' to conceal stowaways. Payment methods were, 'half the amount chargeable is paid to the crew upon leaving Hong Kong: the balance when the stowaways are landed'. The stowaway on landing signed a note which is 'stamped by the storekeeper to whom the stowaway is taken', this is then 'presented in Hong Kong when the balance of the money is paid'. Competition among the various 'syndicates' for the limited places on ships and price cutting led to rivalry and, 'accounts for the letters (anonymous) which have been sent to the Department'.[168] All this was in 1906-8, but stowaways were still being

---

* The Eastern and Australiasian Line.

reported arriving in Sydney in the 1950s and 1960s off ships such as the *Changte*.[169]

Chinese passengers were regulars on the route to Hong Kong

Solidarity?

Those that were caught were not abandoned or ignored by those in Sydney. Stowaways, deserters and other 'prohibited immigrants' who were caught faced gaol terms before they were deported unless someone was willing to go surety until they embarked on a ship back to Hong Kong. This was common with, for example, George Gay and Lee Bung Yee in 1923 doing so for 20 deportees at £50 each for a total of £1,000. The usual bond was £100, but as the number in this case was so large a discount must have applied.[170]

Getting caught was usually a matter of being informed on. (Whatever the reason for informers, if discovered it would be unlikely they would be welcomed. Certainly, George Mook considered it 'a serious thing' when Leong Hoi Cheng, a deportee he interpreted for, accused him of being one.)[171] Lee Fook deserted his ship in 1916 only to be caught in 1930 along with another illegal entrant, Lum Bow. Both were working in a market garden when they were detained by Customs Officers, 'acting on certain information'. They were both given the Dictation Test at the Customs House, Sydney and deported. Their 'tests' were blank, apart from their signatures.*[172] The informer in this case needed to write to the Collector of Customs twice in order to claim her £10 reward per person.[173] Kwok Yen Fong was similarly informed on after successfully remaining in Australia from 1915 to 1933 and having, 'deliberately scarred the tips of his fingers' to escape identification. He continued to show a high level of determination to remain in Australia and managed to escape the Customs Officers. As his file ends at

---

* Despite the Dictation Test being entirely fake, legal proceedings demanded the pretence be thoroughly maintained. A 1927 instruction explained such details as the use of an interpreter to explain what was required, the possibility of authorising an outside person to give the test in the language chosen, the necessity of reading the whole passage at dictation speed even if the person makes no attempt to write, and the fact that it was not allowable to abandon a test started in a language that the person unexpectedly looked like passing.

this point, it could be assumed that Kwok Yen Fong was able to remain in Australia.[174]

The organisation of the various methods of illegal entry, the assistance for those who were caught and the silence of those who knew, are all elements of the historic link between Sydney and south China. This was a link stronger than fear of the law, and in some cases, of the personal risks involved.

Sydney's role as the main access point for illegal entrants emphasises the fact that it was a port and that the Sydney/South China connection at this time was dependent on shipping. Throughout the period, the journeys between Sydney and South China were usually provided by two companies which operated two ships each between Sydney and 'all ports' to either Hong Kong or Yokohama. This meant an average of two ships per month and a trip of about three weeks between Sydney and Hong Kong.♣ For *huaqiao* from the district of Zhongshan at least, the rest of the journey was relatively short, by smaller craft across the Pearl River Delta and then by boat or on foot to and from their villages.♦

♣ See Appendix IV, Table 11 for ship departures from Sydney for 1929.

♦ See Pearl River Delta Map, Chapter 1.

Shipping

At the beginning of the century, shipping companies such as the Eastern and Orient Line and the Taishan Maru operated the *St Albans* and *The Empire*. Later, the Japanese line was replaced by the Eastern and Australian Steamship Co. and the *huaqiao* continued their journeys on ships such as the *Taiping,* the *Tanda* and the *Changte*. These ships were much smaller than those used on the European routes. One of the larger ships on the run, the *Tanda* was 6956 tons and was licensed to carry 258 passengers. In comparison, the *Orion,* which went to Europe via the Suez Canal, was 23,371 tons and carried over 400 passengers.[175]

In 1921, the 'Deck class passage money' on an Eastern and Australian Steamship Co. ship to Hong Kong was £5/10/-.[176] In addition to the cost of passage, the CEDT itself cost £1. For a market gardener this was about three weeks' wages for the ticket, and at least half a week's wage for the CEDT.[177] Including the loss of income while away, this meant that these journeys were an expensive, though necessary, activity for the *huaqiao* if links to the family and village were to be established and maintained.

Huaqiao usually travelled third class or steerage, though 2nd class passage was purchased by merchants and wealthier market gardeners and those travelling with wives and children. People of Chinese origin rarely travelled 1st class in the first half of the twentieth century in these European run ships. [178] In ships such as the *Changte,* 'steerage' was literally the cargo hold, [179] while in the *Nanjing*, 'Special attention will be paid to the accommodation for the Chinese third-class passengers, which will …. [have] full provision for ventilation and electric fans.'[180] All Chinese travelling together did have the advantage at least that the meals served would be Chinese.[181]

The purchase of steamship tickets was another matter handled by the stores, not only in Sydney but also Hong Kong.[182] In this, as in so many matters, the average *huaqiao* had little choice. Shipping agents at the end of the nineteenth century such as Mr Alfred Low preferred not to have to deal with the *huaqiao* directly. He agreed with the Chinese Gambling Commissioners that 'if an ordinary Chinamen came to book a passage they would refuse to take his money; he would have to book through a Chinese merchant'.[183]

The Immigration Restriction Act continued this approach and extended it to Hong Kong and beyond. It did this by fining a shipping company £100 for every illegal immigrant carried to an Australia port. The result was that Chinese people in Hong Kong could not purchase a ticket to

Australia without either a valid CEDT or a letter from the Collector of Customs stating that they would be admitted, 'on being satisfactorily identified'. Ah Pong, when he reported that his CEDT had been stolen in China, needed such a letter before he could return to Sydney, all negotiated via a Sydney store.[184]

```
    With reference to the accompanying papers
respecting the case of Ah Pong whose certificate
exempting from the dictation test, issued in January
last, is said to have been stolen from him in China,
this man may be readmitted  on being satisfactorily
identified.
```

Arrangements necessary to comply with these restrictions appears in the practice, of Zhongshan *huaqiao* at least, of surrendering their CEDTs so that agents could purchase steamer tickets for them. Nearly all the third class passengers on the *Arafura* when it steamed into Sydney in May 1929 had their CEDTs marked 雪梨 [Sydney] on the back, along with the name of the store or agent who arranged the passage, such as 光和丰 (Kwong War Fong) the Hong Kong branch of Philip Lee Chun's Kwong War Chong of 84 Dixon St, Sydney. *Huaqiao* from districts other than Zhongshan did not necessarily operate in the same manner. When the *Taiping* arrived in Sydney in August 1929, the

CEDTs of its 29 *huaqiao* steerage passengers were unmarked, by Chinese characters or anything else, [185]

The stores were able to play this role in buying tickets due to their knowledge of European ways, their ability to communicate in English and the capacity of the managers and merchant's class position to override, to some extent at least, racial bias. The *huaqiao* continued therefore to be dependent upon the stores for all aspects of their dealings with the Act, including filling in forms and answering questions. When Tarm Hew, a vegetable hawker of Botany, was questioned on a discrepancy in his applications, he could only plead that the 'person who filled in my present application … must have misunderstood me'.[186]

Gifts

Despite the various difficulties and costs created by the Act, tens of thousands of *huaqiao* trips were made and those who returned to their villages were expected to bring gifts and to display some of the success they were experiencing in foreign lands. A shopping visit to a local trading store such as the Kwong War Chong or to Anthony Hordern & Sons, was therefore necessary before taking ship. Items purchased included such gifts as Arnott's biscuits and boiled lollies, and necessities such as guns, leather shoes and in at least one instance, an Ajax safe.[187] Arthur Chang remembers the 'biscuits from the new gold mountain' bought at Anthony Hordern and a bird cage his father made from a tea chest in order to hold a rosella he brought back from Australia.[188]

Safe abandoned in a corner of Lee Man Dick's village house.
One of many items regularly brought by *huaqiao* to the villages.
On the name plate can be read where it was purchased.[189]

Children

Sojourns home often resulted in gifts to the family of another kind - children. An event most *huaqiao* would hear about only after they had returned to Sydney. The new child would not usually see its father until it was a few years old and this delay was common enough to have produced, in one Zhongshan village at least, a 'tradition' that on the father's return to the village the 'unmet' child was hidden until everyone else had been greeted and only then introduced.[190] The coinciding of a sojourn in the village with the birth of a child was so common that officials would request the date of all trips or query 'Was he in China about the time of birth,' before proceeding with an application that involved sponsoring children such as that for a student exemption.[191]

The links with the family and village of the *huaqiao* throughout the middle years of their life involved more than purchasing a steamer ticket once every so many years and visiting with gifts or conceiving children. The presence and contribution of the *huaqiao* extended beyond the times when they were physically 'holidaying' in the village. This was because the underpinning of the relationship between Sydney and the villages was the capacity to earn more money in Australia than was possible in the villages or in China generally. The money sent back and the uses to which it was put were material evidence of their hard working contribution to the family and the village.

Land

Life in Australia for those *huaqiao* with continuing links was therefore about earning money and to the majority of rice farming *huaqiao* this meant buying land, considered the most prestigious way to hold wealth. The exchange value between what could be earned in Australia and purchased in south China meant that a relatively poor market gardener in Sydney could purchase sufficient land in his village to make his family very well off.* The proportion of *huaqiao* who were successful in buying land and the proportion who, like John Louie Hoon, were unable to provide for their families in this way, is not possible to determine from Australian sources alone. However, a survey of south China villages taken in the 1930s found up to 90% of farmers to be tenants and that one impact of *huaqiao* remittances was to increase land prices as the *huaqiao* bought more land. The *huaqiao's* large scale investment in land contributed to a spiral of rising land prices and rents which in turn led to debts and the loss of land for those, including presumably poorer *huaqiao*, who could not keep up.[192]

The land purchased was not farmed by the family directly but instead was rented out, possibly to relatives and certainly to fellow villagers.[193] Rent could be paid in cash or as a share of the rice crop and then sold on the highly speculative rice market.[194] Arthur Chang's grandmother received her rent in traditional silver cash, while Cliff Lee's mother collected her rent in kind.[195] The handling of the family's affairs, such as deposits on land, rent collection and payment of taxes, was usually in the hands of the wife.[196]

---

* See Chapter 1 for a comparison of earnings and purchasing power.

Life in the village for the wife and family could be harsh, with health hazards such as the plague, smallpox and cholera being common well into the twentieth century.[197] Opium, prostitution, gambling and syphilis were also part of village life and according to some researchers more likely to be present due to *huaqiao* remittances. Analysis of the role of clan elite's has revealed that they attempted to gather some of the remittance money of the *huaqiao* by demanding money for 'protection' and controlling gambling, opium houses and prostitution.[198]

Nevertheless, for those with land, life in the village could be comfortable. Not all, however, owned land or could save sufficient from their remittances to purchase it. Many families were dependent on remittances for their basic survival and they had little left over for improving their status or long-term prospects. By the 1930s, dependence on remittances seems to have been high in the villages of south China, with the money being spent on food, home, education and ancestors, in that order.[199]

A high level of dependence meant that if the flow of remittances to the family was threatened or broken the result could be the destruction of the family in China or the isolation of the individual in Australia. Chang Yet lost his left thumb when working as a cabinet maker in 1925, resulting in remittances to his family ceasing for many months and his family fearing the worst. He was fortunate in that he received £25 compensation and was able to continue to earn a living.[200] How many were not so fortunate is difficult to know.

The regular flow of remittances into those villages with a significant *huaqiao* element was the norm, however, and the most conspicuous impact on such villages was the building of new and bigger houses by the *huahu* (families of *huaqiao* in the villages). Such a house might include a distinctive 'tower', such as Lee Man Dick and many *huaqiao* built as an addition to a more traditional house, or a totally 'foreign' house built by wealthy *huaqiao* like the Kwoks or Joe Wah Gow.[201] In either case, the contrast with the smaller and more traditional houses in a village was unmistakable.

Joe Wah Gow's house clearly dominates
his village of Long Tou Wan.[202]

Donations

Village and clan loyalty demanded that more be done than just support the immediate family and as *huaqiao* successfully established businesses and became more financially comfortable, their donations to the villages played an important role in *huaqiao* districts.[203] The impact of *huaqiao* donations on Long Tou Wan (龍頭環), the village of Joe Wah Gow, included the building of the 'Joe Song' school with donations from Joe Song, an American *huaqiao* (responsible for the 'Dollar' stores in North America), as well as donations from Joe Wah Gow and others.[204] Apart from schools, Long Tou Wang was considered exceptional in having electricity derived from the rice mill generator which ran an electric water pump. The village also had a covered canal for drainage and a free medical clinic started by Joe Wah Gow and funded with the donations of other *huaqiao*.[205] Arthur Chang remembers a tree being cut down to build a school in his village of Dou Tou (渡頭), made possible largely with donations from *huaqiao* in Hawaii.[206] Norman Lee remembers his father donating money for a village bridge.[207] The village of Zhuxiuyuan (竹秀園), from which the founders of Wing On Company came, was well known to have had running water before most.[208]

Investments

Donations successfully established schools and other village infrastructure. Money in the form of business investments in the home districts were not always so successful. The Kwong War Chong's branches in both Hong Kong and Shekki are examples of some degree of financial success. While in 1924 two Sydney *huaqiao* established the Xiangshan Bank in Shekki which collapsed after two years operation.[209] Lee Yip Fay returned to Sydney in 1928 after a lengthy time spent trying to, 'float The Chosen Co. of Hongkong, Canton and Shakee [Shekki], General Importers and Exporters' of which he was the Manager of the 'Shakee Branch'. Lee Yip Fay reported in words that convey a sense of the personal hardships some *huaqiao* endured that:

'... our Chinese internal trouble caused us no end of worry and suffered heavy losses and was continually harassed in business and my ambitions were scattered, so much so, …. it amounted to an ordeal …'[210]

The impact of the success of such investments on the links between Sydney and south China, had economic and political circumstances been more congenial, can only be a matter of speculation. Lee Yip Fay was trying to encourage officials to make his temporary admission to Australia permanent, nevertheless, he may not have been exaggerating too much when he wrote:

> '… had my plans succeeded, I am confident that I would have been instrumental in opening up new avenues for the exchange of trade with Australia …'[211]

Bandits and other problems

The social disorder in Zhongshan district alluded to by Lee Yip Fay not only limited economic opportunities but was a dramatic background to the life of the 'wife and family' in the 'native country'. In the late nineteenth century and through the first half of the twentieth century these social disorders included numerous attempted anti-Qing Dynasty and republican uprisings, disputes with the Portuguese enclave of Macao, the destruction of tax offices, communist uprisings, land reform movements, provincial border wars, and most commonly and most likely to impact upon even the most isolated villages, bandit attacks.[212]

The threat of 'bandits', usually landless peasants and former soldiers living in the hills and mountains, was a perennial one in Chinese history.[213] However, after the collapse of the Qing Dynasty and the failure of the new Republic to maintain law and order, the threat from bandits greatly increased.[214] Those who lost their land were often forced into banditry and kidnapping to survive. Kidnapping's and other more subtle means of gathering money from *huahu* often left them little better off despite years of remittances.[215] Taxes were also levied on *huahu* for the building of watch towers, the payment of guards and 'black-ticket fees'. This last referred to money paid to local 'bosses' which if not paid led to a 'black-ticket' being issued that would prevent crops being either sown or harvested.[216] Bandits and revolutionaries resulted in similar kinds of disruption for the *huaqiao*, such as during the 1925 Communist attempt to take over Guangdong province, when Arthur Chang's family was forced to flee to the county capital of Shekki. Many Long Dou *huahu* preferred to remain in Shekki after this and generally settled in the suburb of Long On Lee.* The Changs however chose to return to their village.[217]

As the warlord period merged into the anti-Japanese War, governmental order in Zhongshan further collapsed and villages and districts came under the control of local bandit bosses or *Datiener* (大天二),[218] who fought each other for control of territory and the right to levy taxes.[219] A cousin

---

* For more detail on this Australian dominated suburb of Shekki see Mavis Yen, (Siaoman Yen & Richard Horsburgh, eds), *South Flows the Pearl,* (Sydney University Press, 2022).

of Arthur Chang's who was a minor such bandit, was regarded as a protector of the village.[220] Another *Datiener,* known as 'Big Gall Bladder' Hoon, received his name for attending a gathering known to be an ambush, he arrived without bodyguards or weapons with the effect that no one dared to attack him.[221] Such stories repeated 50 years later have a romantic flavour; for Sydney's *huaqiao* and their families in the villages at the time, they must have been merely terrifying.

To protect themselves from these dangers the *huahu* and their neighbours needed to rely on themselves as it was customary for Chinese villages and towns to provide their own security.[222] The villages of Zhongshan varied greatly in size, which meant that they also varied in their capacity to defend themselves. Larger villages, such as Joe Wah Gow's Long Tou Wan, which had a population of 4,000, would protect itself from bandits by electing a 'marshal', surrounding the village with guard towers supplied with 'cannon' and posting four regular guards.[223] Chang Yet's village of Dou Tou was also protected by village 'forts'.[224] Smaller villages, such as Lee Man Dick's Jin Huan, relied on the protection of 'tower' houses built by each *huahu*.[225] While Zhuxiuyuan, the village of the Wing On & Co. founders, being close to the city of Shekki had no need of tower houses or other protective measures.[226] By the time even Shekki came under attack, wealthy families such as the Kwok's of Wing On & Co., had moved to Hong Kong.[227]

A typical tower house built by *huaqiao* for security from bandits. Note the gun holes beside the upper windows.[228]

One common method of coping with the threat from bandits was the building of what are known as 'tower houses' (碉 樓).* Traditional village houses in south China are single

---

* *Diaolou*, or literally fort building or gun tower.

story buildings with, at most, a high roof for storage. Travellers today in the *huaqiao* districts of Zhongshan and the Sze Yap will see numerous villages with many two to three storey 'towers' incorporated into the traditional houses.[*] These towers had gun holes for defence and internal iron barred doors to prevent intruders reaching the upper floors. When not being used for defence they contained bedrooms and served a routine role in the family home.[229]

Despite these hazards of life in the village, for those who sojourned regularly and who did not wish to or could not change the location of the family, there must have been a constant dilemma about whether to remain in the village or to return to Australia. Chang Yet at one point decided not to return to Australia, or even apply for a CEDT until he was convinced by a family friend that he had 13 mouths to feed (including two wives and a slave girl) and 'anything' could happen. The Great Depression did happen and ensured Chang Yet's return in 1933, this time bringing his son Chang Gar Lock (Arthur Chang) with him.[230] Nevertheless, a significant minority of *huaqiao* sought written references, applied for their Certificate exempting them from the

---

[*] Much more elaborate towers in the nearby district of Kaiping are now world heritage listed.

operation of the Dictation Test and paid their £1 in order to ensure that they could return, but did not in fact do so.

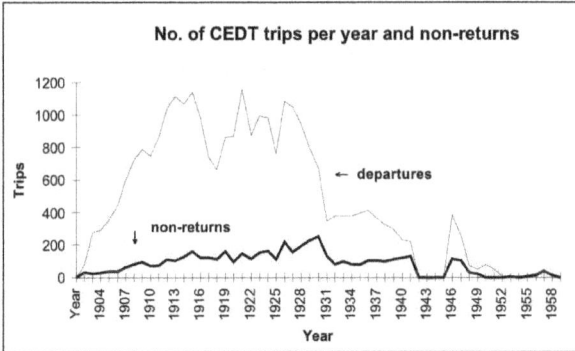

No. of CEDT trips per year and non-returns

Chart 4: The numbers of *huaqiao* making trips dramatically declined after about 1926 as did their total, while the proportion of non-returns increased. At this point the 'domicile' generation were at least 50 years or older. See Appendix IV, Table 10.

Those that did not return may have obtained the CEDT's as insurance just in case all was not well at home. The prevalence of disease and other hazards for the increasingly older men is another possible explanation.[231] The CEDT could also have been obtained in order to pass on to fellow villagers.

Hong Kong

Sydney or the village was not the only choice available for those with some money and despite the many improvements *huaqiao* remittances could bring, village life was not always acceptable or safe, particularly for those who had grown used to something different.[232] For those who could afford not to live in Sydney, and for the increasing number of Australian-born Chinese who felt at home in (or alienated from) both European and Chinese cultures, Hong Kong was the ideal location. Hong Kong had played a significant role as a conduit between the *huaqiao* and their villages ever since the British had taken control of the island in the 1840s. Even while the British and Chinese had tried to ignore each other, Hong Kong had become the base for operations essential to the *huaqiao* links such as buying passage on European ships, sending and receiving remittances, and the return of bones to the villages. In the development of this role for Hong Kong, *huaqiao*, including Australian *huaqiao,* played a major part.[233] Regardless of district, for those with wealth to protect, Hong Kong was a safe haven from both the poverty and corruption of the home villages, and the discrimination and foreignness of Australia.

For families such as the Pan Kees and the Kwoks, regular trips to Hong Kong, the bilingual education of their children and business branches in both Hong Kong and Australia were part of normal life. Thomas Pan Kee of Moree and Narrabri, and later Campbell St Sydney, had 10 children, two born in Hong Kong. During the 1920s all the children were living in Hong Kong while Thomas himself remained in Sydney. In 1930, the whole family returned to live in Sydney. Between 1930 and 1950 various of these children lived in both Hong Kong and Sydney, with most marrying in Hong Kong.[234]

The Pan Kees

Pearl Kwok was Australian-born and left for Hong Kong in 1926, aged 14, marrying there in 1931 one of the Kwoks of Wing On.* She visited her mother in Sydney in 1946 and again in 1949, that time with three of her four children. The entry of these children was refused at first, then later granted temporarily. Pearl and two of her children returned to Hong Kong in 1954 while one daughter, Marina, stayed and became an Australian citizen in 1960.[235]

---

* Nee, Lock Lee of the well-known Alexandria cabinetmakers.

From Hong Kong wealthier *huaqiao* could visit their village when desired, without running the risks humbler *huaqiao* took in living there full time. These risks included not only kidnapping, such as Lee Man Dick suffered, but also the importunity of poorer relations.[236] Joe Wah Gow, on the other hand, despite his wealth was satisfied with returning to his village in 1929 taking with him all his Australian-born children.[237]

Conclusion

The relationship that the *huaqiao* of Sydney had with their 'native country' extended beyond what could be described as 'holiday' visits. The most physical element of the link, after marriage, involved frequent and regular journeys to the village for some, including the arrival of children soon after most trips. In order to take this 'holiday' to see his wife and family, the *huaqiao* had to deal first with the requirements of the Immigration Restriction Act and the barriers that these presented. One of these requirements was that the overall numbers of Chinese in Australia should be seen to be falling. A fall some *huaqiao* slowed by their organised attempts to bring in people in contravention of the Act. These barriers were overcome at the price of continued dependence upon district stores for support, even to the extent of needing them to buy tickets for travel. If moderately successful, a *huaqiao* bought rice farming land for which his wife collected the rents and if more successful he donated money to his village for schools and other improvements. China's social and political disorder, including bandits and civil war, however, stalled any deepening of the connection economically. This disorder also meant that many wealthier *huaqiao* preferred to live outside their home village in places such as the Zhongshan district capital Shekki or in Hong Kong. The preferences of the aging *huaqiao* and of the generation which followed, them in both China and Australia, is the subject of the next chapter.

Edna Lock Lee, unlike her Australian born siblings was born while the family was in Hong Kong. She was given 10 years grace to enter to Australia.[238]

CHAPTER 3

Apart from the native born, the majority are old and weak
除土生者外泰半老弱

In 1939, the manager of Wing On & Co., Sydney wrote to
Chiang Kai Shek to ask him to intervene with the British
government to allow more Chinese people to enter
Australia. He did this because he feared that, 'apart from the
native [Australian] born, the majority are old and weak'.[239]
The old and weak he referred to were the last of the pre-
1901 *huaqiao,* their fellows having either died or made their
final retirement trips to the village. The importance of
finally returning to the village cannot be better illustrated
than by the care that was taken to ensure that the bones of
many that had died in Australia were returned to the
ancestral soil. The majority of 'native born' were of a
younger generation, a generation that also included those
who had come to Sydney after 1901. This succeeding
generation was more limited in its ability to sojourn than the
'domicile' generation and this fact as well as the impact of
war and revolution saw the links with the home districts
transformed.

This chapter begins by describing the changes in the now
older *huaqiao* population as age, death and final retirement
have their impact and the importance of a final return to the

village, even after death, is discussed. After this the growth of a new generation of Sydney *huaqiao* is examined as, despite the intentions of the Immigration Restriction Act, many *huaqiao* have entered Australia in the years after 1901. The categories under which this new generation of *huaqiao* arrived and the influence of restrictions related to these categories in influencing their links with the home villages is considered. Also considered are the Australian-born Chinese who make up a significant proportion of the new generation, and this includes those Australian-born Chinese who were raised in the home villages. Finally, the impact of the Japanese War on the villages and home districts and the nature of the post-war links of the new generation are examined.*

The effect of the Immigration Restriction Act, combined with the location of most *huaqiao* families in the villages, resulted in a steady increase in the average age of Sydney's *huaqiao* population as it fell dramatically in size.* As we have seen, the average age of the *huaqiao* on their arrival in Sydney and NSW was between 16 and 25 years of age.* By

---

* The term 'Japanese War' is used here to include what the Chinese refer to as the anti-Japanese War and what Europeans call the later starting World War Two or Pacific War.

* See Appendix 1, Table 1.

* Chapter 1, Chart 1.

the 1920s, this had risen to their 40s and 50s, and by the 1940s the age of most Chinese market gardeners was such a feature that a visiting Immigration Officer could 'become suspicious of him because of his apparent relative youthfulness'.[240] Of the 58 *huaqiao* passengers arriving in Sydney on the *Arafura* in 1929 from sojourns in the villages, for example, only six were under 50, twenty-five were between 50 and 60 years old, and nineteen, including one aged 71, were over 60.[241]

Final return

The desire to go back to one's home soil was considered in traditional Chinese culture to be as a 'leaf returning to the roots', inevitable and proper.♣ As the *huaqiao* aged, the importance of this tradition meant that an increasing number of *huaqiao* made final retirement trips to the home villages.[242] This can be seen in a gradual increase in the ratio of permanent returns to sojourns which can be traced in the CEDTs issued and the records of whether or not those CEDTs were handed back, as was required on re-entry to Australia.♦

♣ This saying is: 落葉歸根 (luo ye gui gen).

♦ See Appendix III, C, for CEDT related procedures.

Not all *huaqiao* who made the final trip home would be recorded in the CEDT records as many would have returned without bothering to apply for a CEDT once they had decided not to return to Australia. It is difficult to estimate how many *huaqiao* might have returned to the home village without getting a CEDT, but a check of the passenger lists for 1929 reveals that a total of 956 Chinese passengers travelled in that year compared to a total of 801 CEDT holders in the same year. After deducting women and children the total of male Chinese passengers was 936. If allowance is made for those travelling on temporary certificates and passports, then it can be said that in 1929 perhaps 100 *huaqiao* departed Sydney without a CEDT. This number can be added to the 228 who did hold CEDTs but who also did not return to give an indication of the proportion who returned permanently at this period.[243]

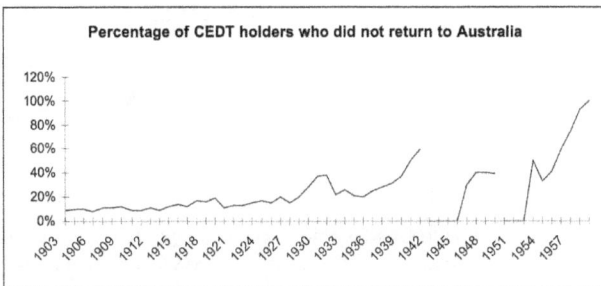

Chart 5: The percentage who did not return remained steady till about 1928, then rose rapidly until the Depression. It began to rise rapidly again about 1936 when the number of trips themselves fell (see Chart 4, Chapter 2). The war stopped all travel and its end saw

a sudden increase which fell again as few 'domiciles' remained. The increase after 1952 is explained by retirees needing a CEDT as a form of Hong Kong entry visa, whether they intended to return or not. See Appendix IV, Table 10.

Some *huaqiao*, perhaps because they had lost all contact with their families in China, did not return to the village. For *huaqiao* in this situation old age in Sydney meant living on their market gardens while they could still work or, if they no longer could work, perhaps in one of the many rooms above Dixon St while earning a little money selling peanuts at Sydney's railway stations and racecourses.[244] John Louie Hoon, for example, lived with about 30 fellow *huaqiao* in the rooms of the Say Tin Co. above Dixon St in Sydney's Chinatown until not long before his death in 1987.♣[245]

For those who died in Sydney before they could return to the villages, it was not necessarily the end of the wish to return to the home village. The practice of returning the bones of the dead to rest in the soil of their ancestors was a fundamental one in Chinese culture and played an important

---

♣ According to Charles Price, based on interview notes made during research conducted in Sydney's Chinatown in the 1970s, the awareness of how many elderly *huaqiao* were living in Sydney, even in the 1970s, was kept from the non-Chinese population of Sydney by ensuring that daily walks were done in pairs to avoid attracting the hostility of white Sydneysiders. Interview with Dr Charles Price, Canberra, 23 February 1998.

role in the bond with the village.[246] This is illustrated in an advertisement that appeared regularly in the *Chinese Australian Herald* (廣益華報) in 1903.[247] It was placed by people concerned about Chinese graves in Townsville whose home villages could not be identified and describes the terrible condition of the ghosts of people who remained apart from their ancestral soil and requests information about the identity of the dead so that their bones can be returned to their villages. The advertisement lists stores in Sydney and Queensland as contact points for passing on the information. The concern of the *huaqiao* that bodies not be lost was so strong that 'the putting of coffins on board vessels going to and fro in case a Chinaman dies' was one of the functions of Sydney's many *huaqiao* societies.[248] Money was also donated to the Tung Wah Hospital in Hong Kong to ensure that this was done at that end also.[249]

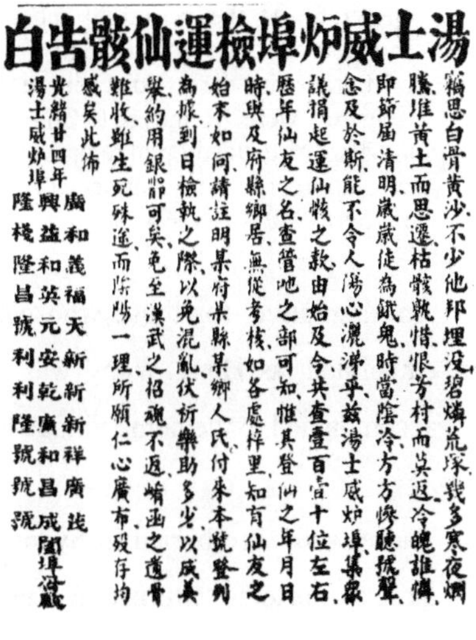
湯士威炉埠檢運仙骸告白

竊思白骨黃沙、不少他邦埋沒、碧燐荒塚、幾多寒夜燗騰、堆黃土而思遷、枯骸孰惜、恨芳村而莫返、冷魄誰憐、即節屆清明、歲歲徒為餒鬼、時當陰冷、方方慘聽號聲、念及於斯、能不令人湯心灑涕乎、茲湯士威炉埠集衆議捐起運仙骸之款、由始及今、共查壹百壹十位左右、歷年仙友之名、查管吔之部可知、惟其登仙之年月日時、與及府縣鄉居、無從考核、如各處梓里、知有仙友之始末如何、請註明某府某縣某鄉人氏、付來本號登列為據、到日檢執之際、以免混亂、伏祈樂助多少、以成美舉、約用銀[illegible]可矣、爰至漢武之招魂不返、嶠函之遺骨難收、雖生死殊途、而[illegible]陽一理、所願仁心廣布、殁存均感矣此佈

光緒廿四年

湯士威炉埠

廣興隆 和益棧 義和隆 福英昌 天元號 新安利 新乾利 新廣隆 祥和號 廣昌號 茂成號

闔埠公啟

Figure 7: 'Notice: exhumation and transport of bones from Townsville.'[250]

Bones rather than bodies are referred to, as the usual practice was to bury a body for several years then to collect the bones of a number of *huaqiao* at once to be 'Removed to China'.[251]

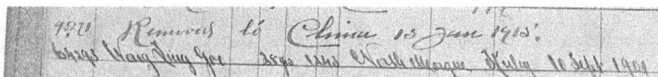

'Removed to China', indicated exhumed plots in the Rookwood Cemetery Chinese Section burial register.[252]

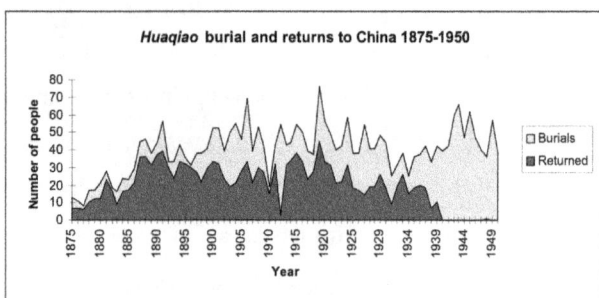

Chart 6: At the period of most active exhumation and shipment of bones, from 1875 to the late 1930s, a peak of 75% of burials in the 'Old Chinese Section' of Rookwood Cemetery were, 'Removed to China', with an average of 55% to 65%. Note the drop in returns around the time of the 1911 revolution. The total number of burials in this section from 1875 to 1950 was 3,094. See Appendix IV, Table 12.

An alternative, for those who could afford it, was to be embalmed, as Hong Wong was in 1901, his body being accompanied to the home village by his sister Ah Ching.[253]

Those who were buried in Sydney sometimes had to wait quite a time to be 'returned to China'. Ah Chung was buried in 1892, but was not returned until 1923, while Ah Sing, who was buried in 1884, was finally removed only in 1946.[254] Another Ah Chung, who died in 1889 aged 23 in Sydney Hospital, must wait indefinitely as his entry is marked, 'Typhoid case not permitted to be removed.'[255] However, the average time in the ground for those whose bones were exhumed was six to seven years, though 10 or 15 years was not unusual. There was a tapering off of returns after 1930, and after 1938 there were very few removals until after World War Two. Many of those who died after 1931 were exhumed between 1946 and 1948, after which only 10 more were removed in 1950, with the last recorded exhumation from this section of Rookwood Cemetery in 1962. [256]

Quong Sin Tong, erected 1877, Old Chinese Section, Rookwood Cemetery, Sydney.

'There is one very old society called Quong Sing Tong.'[257]

The *Tung Wah News* advertisement is another example of services provided by the district stores, but it was the district societies which played the dominant role in the return of bones.[258] The people of the Dung Guan, Zhongshan and Gao Yao districts, who together made up perhaps 60 to 70% of Sydney's *huaqiao,* all had societies which assisted in the return of the bones of the dead.* The societies collected fees from their members and used the funds to ship the bones of those who died in Australia. The Hing Foon Tong (洪福堂) of the Gao Yao people, founded in 1893 by members' subscriptions, kept a membership book which recorded the names and villages of its members to ensure the information would be available when required. [259] The Chinese Gambling Commissioners were told in 1891 that it cost '£10 to remove a man's bones from the country' and that it cost Way Kee's society £529/19/2 to 'raise 84 bodies'.[260] The return of bones to the actual villages was probably done through the Tung Wah Hospital based in Hong Kong, a role this institution played for the *huaqiao* of many countries.[261]

---

* This and support for the return of old men is given as the primary function of all societies referred to in the 1891 *Royal Commission.* See Appendix VI for a discussion of district proportions in Sydney.

The Tung Wah Hospital is still a major institution in Hong Kong
within which nestles the original building with it archives of
bones return. Author picture, 2015.

Next Generation

The *huaqiao* generation which had been resident in Sydney
and NSW since before 1901 were aging, retiring and
shrinking in numbers. Its place was being taken to a smaller
extent in Sydney by a succeeding generation. This
generation was developing in Sydney despite the intentions
of the 1901 Commonwealth Parliament and was made up of
those who entered Australia after 1901 on Certificates of
Exemption, those who were Australian-born and, by the late
1930s, people who can be generally described as 'refugees'.
This last group included Chinese crew members who
refused to return to Japanese held ports in China and

residents of the Pacific islands and New Guinea who were evacuated as Japanese armies advanced.

Between 1902 and 1946 over 6,400 people entered Australia on temporary Certificates of Exemption.♣[262] An estimate of how many of these where able to remain in Australia is that 3,500 had done so by 1947. Though 1,228 of those were relatively recent, having arrived within the previous four years.[263] This would mean that roughly about one in three people who came on a Certificate of Exemption were able to remain permanently.♦ The numbers of Australian-born Chinese also rose significantly over the same period. There were 1,456 Australian-born Chinese in 1911 when they are first distinguished in the Commonwealth Census, rising to 3,728 by 1947. The figures for 'refugees' are less clear as these were also given Certificates of Exemption. However, between the Census of 1933 and that of 1947, the numbers of China-born people in Australia rose greatly with, as already stated, 1,228 arriving since about 1943.[264]

♣ See Appendix III, C for a description of Certificates of
   Exemption.
♦ See Table 13. Appendix IV.

What these figures mean is that by 1947 the breakdown of the *huaqiao* population of Australia and proportionally in Sydney, was roughly as follows:

Huaqiao in 1947	Australia	Sydney(25%)	Proportions
Australian-born Chinese	3,728	931	40.75%
Post-1901 Certificates of Exemption	2,272	568	24.83%
Pre-1901 'Domiciles'	1,921	480	21.00%
Refugees (arrivals within 4 years)	1,228	307	13.42%
Total	9,149	2,286	100.00%

These figures are a rough guide only as many 'refugees' would have arrived since 1939 and so the Certificate of Exemption category is overstated and that of refugees understated. Similarly, the proportions for Sydney are not exact as refugees would have been more likely to have entered and remained there. Nevertheless, these figures give an indication as to the make-up of the generation that succeeded the 'domicile' generation by the end of the Japanese War.

More than 2,000 people entered Australia on Certificates of Exemption and managed to remain until war-time conditions made their return impossible or at least politically difficult. These people entered under various categories and conditions of the same Act that granted CEDTs to their father's generation. They entered as

101

students, merchants, the wives of merchants, and as substitutes and assistants to those working in stores and market gardens.

While the children of *huaqiao* who were born in China generally had no right to enter Australia, it was possible (and this almost always meant sons) to gain temporary entry for study. 'Student' was defined variously, in 1912 it was a minimum of 17 years, then no age limit in 1920, this was replaced with a minimum of 14 and a max of 19 years in 1924. Finally, the age was dropped to 10 years in 1926 when attendance at approved private schools was required.[265] The conditions of the temporary 'Certificate of Exemption' issued in such cases appear to have been strictly adhered to in the early administration of the Immigration Restriction Act.[266] Ah Wang of Forbes, was one of the first to take advantage of the student provisions of the Act.[267]

Using a local land agent rather than a Chinese store to assist him, Ah Wang inquired how he might bring his son Yut Ming, aged 14, to Australia as a student. Despite being refused twice, he was granted permission in January 1909 for his son Yut Ming to study for two years in Australia after entering a £100 bond. When a local police report stated that Yut Ming was not attending school at Eugowra, his Certificate of Exemption was cancelled. Ah Wang then wrote personally to explain that his son had been 'disobedient' but with more English he was now willing to go to school. A delay in the police delivering the deportation order due to 'droving stolen sheep' and the intervention of a local MP resulted in a six month postponement in the decision to deport. Regular police reports confirming that Yut Ming was at school and well behaved led to his certificate being extended. Yut Ming finally sailed for China on the *Eastern*, in May 1911.[268] What advantage Yut Ming derived from his schooling in Australia and whether this was all his father had hoped, can only be speculated upon.

Cliff Lee was also brought to Australia as a student by his father Lee Man Dick in 1949, this being the second time Lee Man Dick had sponsored a son. In 1924, Cliff Lee's brother, Ting Hoy, had come to Sydney, but after reports that 'Lee Ting Hoy has been seen about the city a good deal and appears to be a lad who would be much better off attending school,' he had been required to return to China.[269] Cliff Lee was more fortunate than his brother in being able to change his 'status' from student to that of a market garden assistant, thus enabling him to remain indefinitely in Australia.[270] The differing treatment of these two brothers illustrates the changes in the administration of the Certificates of Exemption as the war and then the new government in

China made the option of deportation an increasingly difficult one for both administrators and politicians.

Helping in the Garden

While the entry of students became gradually more common, a more dramatic change occurred with the exemptions for 'substitutes and assistants'. [271] Under the Immigration Restriction Act, a person could enter Australia either as a 'substitute' for a 'domiciled' *huaqiao* who was returning for a long period or permanently, or as an 'assistant' to help in a recognised 'Chinese' occupation such as a market garden or Chinese store. In the early period of the Act such exemptions were rare and of limited flexibility, such as when Charley Ah Min's son was allowed to come and assist in his father's Binnaway store, but only for six months and with a guarantee that no extensions would be asked for. [272] Ensuring that Chinese numbers did not increase was a great concern for officials, as when Wong Ka Yee was allowed to enter for 12 months as an assistant to replace Mar Chat, and administrators were careful to see that he left within 3 months of Wong Ka Yee's arrival. [273] Occupations that were not seen as 'Chinese', or where competition with 'white' businesses occurred, such as cabinet making, were not able to bring in replacements. Exemptions for market gardeners, on the other hand, became easier as it was recognised that most of Sydney's vegetables were grown by *huaqiao* and that this was endangered by their aging.[274] The NSW Chamber of Fruit and Vegetable Industries supported the transfer in status of Cliff Lee from student to assistant because,

As you know, this Chamber is very concerned at the low production of vegetables and is anxious to do anything it can to improve the supply, and therefore supports the application ...to enable the youth to be employed in the garden.[275]

The substitute and assistant provisions required the need for them to be demonstrated. This was interpreted in terms of turnover and a judgement that the position required a Chinese person to do it. This in turn meant that those with businesses were in a better position to bring family members, or at least fellow villagers, than the average *huaqiao* market gardener.[276] When the *Chinese World News*, the newspaper of the Chinese Masonic Society, applied for Louey Kee Fong to work as a Chinese compositor, the fact that he would, 'not keep a local man out of employment' was significant.[277] Stores such as Kwong War Chong & Co. needed to import goods into Australia as well as to sustain a certain turnover in order to be allowed to employ assistants. In 1933-4, this store imported goods worth over £1,780 and paid duty of more than £1,791. Once a month, salted vegetables, tinned fish, bean curd and ginger were imported on the *Changte*, *Taiping* and the *Tanda*, the same ships that carried the *huaqiao* between Sydney and China. In 1948, the Kwong War Chong, with a turnover of £5,994, was able to employ four assistants.[278]

This link between eligibility to remain in Australia and employment meant that many of those who entered Australia under 'Certificates of Exemption' after 1901 were little better than bonded employees vulnerable to exploitation.[279] This was in a sense a continuation of the pattern of the credit-ticket system.* The freedom to sojourn was also much less than that enjoyed by *huaqiao* with 'domicile' rights and even less if the employment was not secure.♦ Yuk Kwan's employment history illustrates both the greater restrictions faced by those on Certificates of Exemption and the changing administration of the Act in the years during and after World War Two.

Yuk Kwan came to Australia in 1926 to work for the Chinese language newspaper the *Chinese Republican News,* as a compositor. In 1934, his employers wrote to the

---

* See Chapter 1, for examples of 'indentures' given to the Chinese Gambling Commissioners.
♦ No figures are available on trips by those on Certificates of Exemption. Their files are usually about getting extensions and rarely about taking a trip unless leaving permanently.

Collector of Customs that it was 'our intention to dispense with his services', and a week later that they 'will make arrangements for him to leave Australia by the *S.S. Nankin*'. A few days after this the Collector discovered that Yuk Kwan did not intend leaving quietly when the solicitors, 'Pigott, Stinson, Macgregor and Palmer', informed him that a writ had been served on the paper claiming £745/11/-, and requesting, as the court case was some months away, that an extension be granted. The *Chinese Republican News* responded that, 'as this man refuses to leave ... we now disclaim any further responsibility for his stay in Australia'. Yuk Kwan was given a four month extension and in that time was able to find a job with the Chinese Masonic Society newspaper, the *Chinese World News*, where he replaced Yuen Yet Choy, who was returning to China. By April 1935, Yuk Kwan was again in a form of 'bonded' employment.

This was not the end of Yuk Kwan's difficulties and several years later, in 1942, the *Chinese World News* ceased publication and Yuk Kwan needed to find another job. By this time manpower shortages meant that, for the first time since his arrival in Australia 16 years previously, Yut Kwan could take any employment he wished, finding a position with the engineering department of Airlines of Australia. In 1947, with the war over and labour shortages ended, Yuk

Kwan was told that as he was 'not eligible to remain in Australia to continue in his present occupation, arrangements should be made for him to leave the Commonwealth by the first available vessel'. Yuk Kwan showed similar resourcefulness when faced with deportation again and his case appeared prominently in the newspapers. This publicity did not alter the decision to deport but he was granted a six month extension to stay in Australia in order to 'find suitable employment'. This Yuk Kwan was able to do, becoming a waiter and later a supervisor and partner in the Taiping Cafe.

Yuk Kwan, now referred to in his file as Ken Wong, continued to battle with administrators over improving his status. He was finally granted permanent residence in 1959, after various friends certified that he was 'a very good type' and 'has adopted the Australian way of life'. Ken Wong married an Australian-born Chinese person, Edith Olive Edna Quay, and applied for and was granted citizenship in 1960. The final entries in his file report the couple planning a honeymoon to Hong Kong, Japan, France and England, which would have been Yuk Kwan's first trip out of Australia since his arrival 34 years earlier.[280]

Yut Kwan illustrates the difficulties for those of the post 'domicile' generation who were only able to live in

Australia under the conditions of the temporary Certificates of Exemptions. Yut Kwan may have had his personal reasons for not visiting China after his arrival in 1926, but even had he wished to do so, he would have found it extremely difficult to maintain the kind of sojourning undertaken by the 'domicile' generation. Apart from his dependence upon his employers, the temporary nature of his 'Certificate of Exemption' meant there was no guarantee he would be allowed back to Australia. A consequence of this was that links to the home villages were weakened or, as appears to have been the case with Yut Kwan, extinguished entirely.

Yut Kwan was able to marry an Australian-born Chinese woman, something members of his generation were more able to do. However, Australian-born Chinese, whose numbers totalled 3,728 in the Commonwealth Census of 1947, do not represent all people of Chinese origin who were born in Australia. Under pre-Federation NSW law, the children and wives of naturalized Chinese were exempt from the £100 poll tax and could enter freely. The Immigration Restriction Act, on the other hand, recognised the Australian, or rather 'British' citizenship of those naturalized in NSW, but not the rights of their children. A naturalized person such as Sing Kee, for example, was told in 1903 that his children could only be admitted under 'para

(A) of s.3 of the Immigration Restriction Act', that is under the Dictation Test, or in other words, they would not be admitted.[281]

Stating admission was under 'paragraph A of Section 3' was bureaucratic code for refusal, as this was the Dictation Test provision - a fake test that no one passed.

For children who were born in Australia but raised in China
the position was similar legally to that of Sing Kee's
children, though they were in fact often treated better in
practice. The main factor here was a High Court ruling that
stated citizenship was dependent upon 'domicile' and that
such 'Domicile [could be] considered abandoned through
long absence'. [282] The administrators of the Immigration
Restriction Act considered an absence of 'say ten years' as
a rule of thumb in determining such cases but were not
consistent in its application.[283] The overseas born daughter
of Mrs Thomas Pan Kee, for example, had no difficulty
entering Australia in 1922, though the fact that she had eight
Australian-born siblings may have been a deciding factor.[284]
Pearl Kwok was also Australian-born and at one stage was
told that she needed to return by the end of 1926 or she
would not be able to return at all. Pearl Kwok chose to return
much later in the 1930s and had no trouble entering
Australia, though all her children by her Hong Kong based
husband were at first refused entry and later granted only
temporary entry. [285] Joe Wah Gow's sons, who had left
Australia in 1929, had no trouble re-entering, the last, Victor
Gow, did so just as the Japanese were occupying southern
China in 1940.[286]

There could be other limitations to the rights of Australian-born people, including the continued lack of right to citizenship. When Shelia Gock Ming, who was Australian-born and largely brought up in China and Hong Kong, wished to enter Australia she was granted permission as long as, 'she does not marry a person domiciled outside the Commonwealth'.[287] In determining how these restrictions were to be imposed the distinction of 'half-caste' was a significant factor, though inspectors must have had some difficulties when they were instructed, 'If the passengers … are obviously less than half-caste … they need not be restricted at all,' and for '3/4 caste Chinese' a permit was 'not necessary'. Class was an associated consideration with 'slightly coloured passengers of superior standing' also to be unrestricted.[288]

It is difficult to estimate how common it was for Australian-born children to be taken to the villages to be raised while the father returned to Australia. The files show a number of examples of young men returning to Australia who left when children, and the 1929 outgoing ships passenger lists show at least three children under the age of three years travelling in steerage, where they could only have travelled with their fathers.[289]

Billy Chee Hoon was born in Sydney in 1885 and taken to

his father's village when aged nine. He returned to Sydney aged 17 and worked there and later in Glenn Innes as a storekeeper. [290] Similarly, John Louie Hoon was born in Sydney and taken home by his father when aged seven. [291] Both of these people were Australian born, but neither citizenship laws nor attitudes regarded them as Australian or British subjects. Instead, they were subjected to

Billy despite his Australian birth looked far too Chinese to avoid needing to apply for an exemption from the Dictation Test.

the same regulations as *huaqiao* born in various south China villages. Some *huaqiao* took back to the village not only their children but their non-Chinese wife. Again, numbers who may have done this are unknown but they were sufficient to have inspired a circular in 1911 entitled, 'White wives of Chinese and their children'.*[292]

---

* The purpose of the circular was to warn women before leaving that nothing could legally be done if their husbands died and they wished to return to Australia with their children against the wishes of the husband's family.

The Australian-born Chinese, whether raised in Australia or China, and those on Certificates of Exemption in Sydney received a sudden increase in numbers when refugees began to enter Australia as the result of Japan's war in China and the Pacific. Some were Chinese crew members who refused to return to Japanese held areas and others were residents of the many Pacific islands evacuated in the face of the Japanese advance. Still others included those with Australian birth such as Victor Gow and Pearl Kwok who were able to leave Hong Kong and the villages on the approach of the Japanese.[293]

This extension of the Japanese war beyond China not only brought in more *huaqiao* to Sydney but significantly affected the links the last of the old *huaqiao* had with their families in the villages. In 1941, the *Tanda* turned back because of Japan's attack on Pearl Harbour and the invasion of Hong Kong. All Chinese on board, including Leong Hoi Cheng, a ships deserter from 1938 who had just been deported after he was detected working in a market garden, were permitted to 'remain under exemption'.[294] The *Tanda* was the last ship to attempt to take *huaqiao* to their villages. From November 1941 until 1945, not a single CEDT was issued to a Chinese person.[295]

The Japanese invasion not only prevented *huaqiao* from visiting their families, it also cut off those already in the villages from returning. The Japanese invasion of southern China in 1937 caused many people in the nearby districts to flee to Hong Kong from which those that could came to Australia. Those that could not, generally returned to their villages after the Japanese, in 1942, also invaded Hong Kong.[296] *Huaqiao,* such as John Louie Hoon, who had left Australia to go to their villages after the Japanese had invaded China itself, could not return once Hong Kong was invaded.[297] Billy Gay relates that John Louie Hoon and his family at one point were reduced to eating grass and how on several occasions John Louie Hoon was struck by Japanese soldiers with rifle butts for not being quick enough to bow.[298]

The invasion of Hong Kong also meant that remittances could no longer be sent through stores and agents based there. This drastically reduced the flow of money to the villages when the *huahu* needed it most. [299] Some remittances did continue to get through, smuggled via the Chinese wartime capital of Chungking, but deprived of most of their remittances and suffering the disruptions of war many *huahu* suffered greatly.[300]

With the end of the war, Sydney's links with south China did not return to its pre-war condition. The Kuomintang government, even before the end of the war, had begun channelling remittances through the Bank of China, cutting out the many district stores that had performed this task since the nineteenth century. [301] The new Communist government also encouraged remittances and also accepted them only through the Bank of China.[302]

These changes, combined with the increased number of Australian-born Chinese and the final return of the last of the domiciles who still wished to do so brought about the end of the link between Sydney and south China as it had existed for more than half a century. [303] Hong Kong remained as a refuge for many and a continuing source of new arrivals to Australia, often as 'cafe assistants'.[304] Many Sydney residents had relatives in the new China and were anxious for news and opportunities to bring them out, but were less inclined or able to visit them than in the past. Arthur Chang, at one stage, used the well known New Zealand supporter of the new Chinese Government, Rewi Alley, to carry a letter to his family and Donald Young remembers regularly receiving closely typed news sheets from Hong Kong about his and other families from his district.[305]

Some of the very few older *huaqiao* who remained in Sydney continued to return. Lee Man Dick returned in 1956 aged 69, dying in that same year.[306] Young Sing, who had

been working in Australia since 1895 and made eight sojourns and fathered three children, made his final trip back to the village aged 75 in 1955.[307] Perhaps the last *huaqiao* to return by the old methods before the abolition of the Dictation Test in 1958, was Sun Lee aged 77, who departed in 1958 on a Qantas flight, having been in Australia since 1898.[308]

Sun Lee

For the succeeding generation, the generation that in a sense did not return, the links to south China, while not ended, were of a different nature. For people such as Arthur Chang, Cliff Lee and Victor Gow, the link was a matter of efforts to bring remaining family members to Australia, or of nostalgic visits in later years.* Cliff Lee, for example, returned to China to visit his mother, after his father died in 1957, entering through Macao and leaving again the same

---

* For an exploration of the link as heritage see *Heritage and History in the China-Australia Migration Corridor* (HKU Press, 2023).

way. He helped to set up his mother and two sisters-in-law in Macao before returning to Sydney. At the end of the 20th century Cliff Lee had investments in Zhongshan and lived in Shekki (now Zhongshan City), for part of every year.[309] Victor Gow, a son of Joe Wah Gow, also had interests in Zhongshan, in a joint venture business which imported air conditioner parts into Australia.[310] A further stage in the links occurred in 1981 when Louie Yick Cheong, manager of Hong Sings in Dixon St and a member of the Chinese Masonic Society, helped to bring John Louie Hoon's youngest daughter, She Fang to Australia.[311] John Louie Hoon now has a grandson in Sydney with no doubt as to his Australian citizenship.

Australian born John Louie Hoon with his
China born daughter, She Fang.

Conclusion

For anyone with a memory of the *huaqiao* numbers earlier in the century, as the manager of Wing On & Co., Sydney probably did when he wrote that, 'apart from the native [Australian] born, the majority are old and weak', the numbers by 1939 were cause for concern. Age and the desire to return to the ancestral soil meant that the majority of the older *huaqiao* had made their final retirement trips to the villages by the middle of the century. The custom of bones return ensured that many of those who died in Sydney also returned to the home villages. Despite this decline, however, and the operation of the Immigration (Restriction) Act a new generation of *huaqiao* established itself in both Sydney and Australia. This generation was made up of those who entered Australia after 1901 on Certificates of Exemption and were able to remain long enough to take advantage of changes in attitudes and laws, an increasing number of Australian-born Chinese who were either brought up in Australia or if in China were not considered to have lost 'domicile', and towards the end of the 1930s, an increasing number of refugee arrivals. This emerging generation maintained links with the villages and home districts distinct from those of the pre-1901 *huaqiao* but sufficient to ensure that the historical links between Sydney and the villages and districts of south China were not lost.

119

CONCLUSION
No further action will be taken

In 1956, Immigration Department officials marked Lee Man
Dick's file 'no further action will be taken'.[312] They did this
because on his final return to Zhongshan, Lee Man Dick
ended their interest in him by selling his Rockdale Fruit and
Vegetable shop, not to other *huaqiao* or even to his son in
Sydney, but to Italian migrants. In making that comment the
officials were acting, perhaps unknowingly, within a history
of bureaucratic monitoring of the links between Sydney and
the villages of south China that had been in existence for
over half a century.

This work began by referring to the presence in south China
villages of objects such as the Anthony Hordern & Sons
safe, of a village medical clinic founded with money earned
in Wollongong, and of the puzzlement over the 'apparent'
citizenship of an Australian-born person. If this history has
contributed to an understanding of how such things came to
be, then it has achieved part of its aim. This work has also
aimed to contribute to that process of disaggregation of the
history of the Chinese in Australia referred to by Henry
Chan,[313] as well as to place that history more clearly within
the context of south China. For this purpose, the term
huaqiao has been used in preference to 'Chinese' and the

'Chinese community' in order to identify those people of Chinese birth and origin whose story is the subject of this history. In adopting this usage some of the complexities that exist beneath these terms has perhaps been demonstrated, along with the need for greater care in their use.

The history of the relationship the *huaqiao* maintained between Sydney and south China, from the late nineteenth century to the middle of the twentieth century, has been traced along the lines of the life patterns of the *huaqiao*, from youth through marriage and family, into old age, retirement and onto the next generation. In using such an approach, the aim has been to focus on the perspective's most significant to the *huaqiao* themselves and to attempt to provide some balance to the bias inevitably resulting from reliance on sources created by discriminatory legislation.

This approach has assisted in revealing that the majority of Sydney *huaqiao* maintained links with the villages and districts of south China, and that these links centred on the need to support their families in those villages. The young 'new chum' *huaqiao* were able to mature and grow old in Sydney as residents and workers while also becoming landowners and heads of village households in China. Such a pattern was supported by stores and societies organised around the district of origin, confined by the administration

121

of the Immigration Restriction Act and sustained by the presence in the villages of parents, wives and children.

Naturally variations in this basic pattern existed. Some *huaqiao* never had any links to their villages, or lost them over time. Others stopped sojourning early to settle in the village, or were prevented from sojourning by decisions under the Immigration (Restriction) Act. Still others married in Australia and either did not maintain links or perhaps began a process of weakening them by using Hong Kong as a safer place to live and educate their children. Many of these variations were based on the opportunities opened by money and class position. It is difficult to say what proportion of *huaqiao* may have followed these alternatives but it is reasonable to say that the majority of *huaqiao* who were granted 'domicile' in 1901 followed the primary pattern outlined by this history.

Particular features of this basic relationship are worth noting. Primary among them was a strong desire by most *huaqiao* to return to their village. This saw many make a final retirement trip in their old age as well as support a system for returning the bones of their district fellows who died before they could make such a trip. Attempts to bring people into Sydney in defiance of the legislation is a further interesting feature of the link. One feature that is not considered in great detail here emphasises the personal level on which the links with the villages and districts operated. This was the presence in the villages of unknown numbers of Australian-born children and 'white' wives.

Many questions remain unanswered and the need for further study in several areas is clear. Of most interest and potential reward is the need for study in the villages of south China, including oral history research, in order to provide a more detailed picture about such questions as the 'success rate' of those who returned, or to fill the frustrating gap in our knowledge about those women who remained in the villages. Those who, while living in fear of bandits and other hazards, collected rents and looked after parents and children.*

Sydney has been identified in this history as the centre of a *huaqiao* business and support network. It was also seen to be the city in which an increasing proportion of *huaqiao* lived as their total numbers in NSW and Australia declined during the first half of the twentieth century. This position of Sydney in *huaqiao* history, as well as the presence of *huaqiao* representatives from a wide range of Pearl River Delta districts, gives the Sydney researcher many

---

* This unfortunately has not been done.

opportunities for comparative work. Research between the people of various Pearl River Delta districts, both within Sydney and between Sydney and other Australian *huaqiao* communities should give most exciting results.

Much of the evidence here was derived from the administrative files of the Immigration Restriction Act. These files have captured much evidence about an entire generation at a point when they were going about, what was for them, an ordinary part of their life. These files not only provide broad evidence of peoples' ages, numbers of trips and the length of time spent in Australia or China, but the careful reading of individual files and examination of the incidentals of lives drawn together by bureaucratic imperatives, along with the comments of officials, enables us to obtain a view into the lives of what one Customs Official described as the 'ordinary vegetable class'[314] of *huaqiao*. Ordinary people who in the usual course of their lives leave scant records for researchers.

Brief Sojourn in your Native Land has attempted to contribute to an understanding of the lives of a unique and almost forgotten group of Sydney residents. It is hoped that a fuller appreciation of the importance of the districts of origin to the *huaqiao*, of the significance of restricted marriage choices and changing conditions in China, of the maturing of a succeeding generation and of the impact of the Immigration Restriction Act, 1901 and its administration has been an outcome of this research. It is also hoped, above all, that a contribution has been made to a clearer knowledge of that pattern of choices and activities, dominated by the desire of the *huaqiao* to support their families in the home villages, that resulted in a history of intimate links between south China and Sydney.

APPENDIX I

Chinese language considerations

Many systems for the romanisation of the many Chinese languages and their dialects[315] have been employed in the past and so much confusion results when texts from different periods are used. 'Mandarin', which is the national language of the People's Republic of China, has had numerous romanisation systems developed to enable it to be pronounced phonetically. Some of the most common are Wade, Yale, Giles, Wade-Giles and finally *Pinyin*, which is that officially used by the Chinese Government today. However, for the Cantonese language, its sub-dialects and non-Cantonese languages such as that spoken within the Long Du area of Zhongshan few or no standard romanisation systems have been developed.

As neither the *huaqiao*, nor the various English speaking officials seeking to write down their names, would have known any such systems, the result was a variety of renderings into English script of the names of people and places. Thus, Zhongshan (using its *Pinyin* romanisation in mandarin pronunciation) was usually written either Chungshan or Chongshan and either variation is recognised by *huaqiao* descents today. When it comes to personal names, however, there are even more complications.

As Philip Lee Chun, whose Chinese name was Lee Lum
Chun though he'd been naturalized as a NSW citizen under
the name Ah Tchee, conceded:

> 'I can readily understand that the Chinese system of
> nomenclature is rather bewildering to a European.'[316]

Many Australians of Chinese descent today carry family
names such as Hoon, Gay and Gooey which have no relation
to traditional Chinese family names. These names usually
derive from the personal names of the first family member
to arrive in Australia.

The explanation for such renderings is a combination of the
non-phonetic basis of written Chinese, language and dialect
variations within spoken Chinese and different cultural
practices in the way family and personal names are given
and written. The absence of a consistent system of spelling
English renderings and a lack of interest in 'getting it right'
on the part of the officials writing them down are
contributing factors.

When, for example, John Louie Hoon's father, Louie Hoon,
gave his name he was expressing his family name Louie
(雷) and his personal name Hoon (寬) in the Chinese order.
Europeans, however, considered 'Hoon' to be the family

127

name. Both 'Louie' or 'Louey' and 'Hoon' were roughly
rendered English phonetic equivalents of the characters 雷
宽 in the Min language of his Long Du area in the district of
Zhongshan.♣ When his son was born, he was given the
English name John, though usually called Jack, and this was
appended to his father's name to make him John Louie
Hoon in the files of the Customs and Excise Office of NSW.
He was also given a Chinese name which began with his
family name Louie (雷) and then Jer (则). This last was
chosen either because it sounded similar to John (or Jack) or
visa versa. As an added twist, John Louie Hoon's fellow
Chinese might ignore his Chinese name and attempt to write
his 'English' name in Chinese characters. The result, 则雷
宽 or Jer Louey Hoon was a confused mix of naming
conventions.[317]

John Louie Hoon and his father were relatively unusual,
however, in referring to their family name at all. The
majority of villagers when asked their name for the purposes
of registration or CEDT applications would omit what, for
English speakers would be the essential element, the family
name. This was not because it was thought unimportant, but
because it was too important. For most Chinese speakers at

♣ These same characters would be written Lei Ze in *pinyin* when
romanising their mandarin pronunciation.

the end of the nineteenth century the 'family' name was the clan or lineage name. They were members of a specific clan but were not in the habit of using that name as part of their personal identification. Such a use was all the more unlikely given that most *huaqiao* would have come from either single surname villages, or villages that had at most, 3 to 4 separate clan names. In such a situation, the habit of using a 'family' name as a personal identifier would not have been very practical.

The result of all this was that when giving his name to a Customs official in the port of Sydney, the average *huaqiao* simply gave his personal name. Yuk Kwan's family name, for example, was Wong, a name that does not appear in his files until the 1950s, some 30 years after the file began, when he also begins to refer to himself as Ken.[318] If a name happened to sound similar to an English name or word then that was written down, such as with Young or Lee. Otherwise a name was rendered as best the differences in basic sounds between the two languages allowed, such as Duck or Dick for 德, and Yet or Yat for 日.

Another common variation also came about when a person had only a single character for their personal name. In this case, it was usual to extend it and make it sound more 'polite' by adding another sound to the beginning. For those of the Pearl River Delta districts this was invariably the sound 'ah' (亞). Sufficient people became known as Ah something, Ah Moy, Ah Yat, etc, that the second and subsequent custom-made alphabetical CEDT registers ordered by NSW Customs had additional leaves tagged 'AH' inserted between the 'A' and 'B' leaves to facilitate their being recorded.[319]

The final factor adding confusion to this issue is that a *huaqiao*'s name might have been different when a boy or young man (that is, before marriage) from that later in his life. As Philip Lee Chun explained, for the benefit of the Collector of Customs, when a son is born, 'the mother gives him a name; when he goes to school, the schoolmaster gives him a name; if the boy marries, then he takes his paternal name…' 'The names given to him in his infancy are of no import, except the family name. It is when he marries that he acquires a definite name.' [320] This was the Chinese practice, but the imperatives of bureaucratic documentation meant that the name of 'no import' often became a *huaqiao's* permanent name. Philip Lee Chun himself was writing this explanation because the Collector of Customs wanted to know why he was claiming to be the naturalized Ah Tchee, the name he used before his marriage.

Chinese characters

This table lists some of the variations in romanisation of Chinese words and names referred to in the text.

Character (former name)	Pinyin Mandarin	Wade-Giles Mandarin	Cantonese (former name)	Other dialect or non-standard romanisation
中山 (香山 or 香邑)	Zhongshan (Xiangshan or Xiang Yi)	Chung Shan (Hsiang Shan or Hsiang I)	Chungshan (Hsiangshan or Hsiang Yap)	Chongshan (Heängshang Heong Shang Hung Shang)
隆都	Long Dou	Long Tou	Lung Dou	Loong Doo
石岐	Shiqi	Shi Ch'i	Shekki	Shakee
四邑	Siyi	Ssu I	Sze-Yap	Ssu Yap See Yip
台山 (新寧)	Taishan (Xinning)	T'ai Shan (Hsin Ning)	Toisan (Sunning)	(Sun Wing)
開平	Kaiping	K'ai Ping	Hoi Ping	Hoy Ping
新會	Xinhui	Hsin Hui	Sunwui	Sun Wiy
恩平	Enping	En Ping	Enping	Ying Ping
三邑	Sanyi	San I	Sam Yap	Sam Yip
翻浴	Fanyu	Fan Yu	Pan-yu	Par Yoon
南海	Nanhai	Nan-hai	Nan-hai	Namhoy
順德	Shunde	Shun-te	Shuntak	Sun Duck
東莞	Dong Guan	Tung Guan	Doon Goon	Toon Goon
增城	Zeng Cheng	Tseng Ch'un	Cheng Sing	Chang Sing
高有	Gao Yao	Kao Yao	Go You	Go Yiu
和山	He shan	Ho Shan	Hao Shan	Hock Sang
客家	Kejia	K'er Chia	Hakka	Har Kar
廣州	Guangzhou	Kwang Chou	Kwangchou	
廣東	Guangdong	Kwangtung	Kwang Tung	Canton
廣善堂	Guangshantang	Kuangshantang	Quong Sin Tong	Quong Sing Tong

APPENDIX II

Oral sources - Interviewees

Oral sources were used to provide much of the evidence of this history. In all seven descendants of Zhongshan *huaqiao* were interviewed. These were:

- **Cliff Lee** entered Australia as a student in 1949 aged 12. Cliff is the second son of the second wife of Lee Man Dick, market gardener and storeowner. Contacted through Dr Shirley Fitzgerald and interviewed in Sydney, 28 September 1997 and in Zhongshan, January 1998.

- **Arthur Gar-lock Chang** also entered Australia as a student, in 1936 aged 14. Arthur is the son of the Chang Yet. Met at a conference on Chinese Australian history and interviewed in Sydney, 28 October 1997.

- **Donald Young** entered Australia as a student in 1949. Donald is the son of an Hawaiian *huaqiao* and the grandson of a Queensland *huaqiao*. Met through Arthur Gar-lock Chang and interviewed in Sydney, 11 October 1997.

- **Victor Gow** was born in Wollongong in 1922 and returned with his father, Joe Wah Gow, to his village in 1928, where he grew up, returning to Sydney in 1940. Met through Donald Young and interviewed in Sydney, 30 October 1997.

- **King Fong** is the son of Fong Say Tin who came to Australia from Fiji and owned the Say Tin Co. in Sydney. Interviewed in Sydney, 1 April 1998.

- **Billy Gay** is an Australian-born Chinese who spent three years as a teenager in his father's village in the 1930s. Billy is the son of George Gay a well known Sydney Market Gardener and a cousin of John Louie Hoon. Met when researching possible Sydney relations of John Louie Hoon and interviewed in Sydney, 19 March 1998.

- **Norman Lee** is one of five sons of Philip Lee Chun a well-known Sydney merchant. He only briefly visited his father's village. Contacted through Dr Shirley Fitzgerald and interviewed in Sydney, 25 September 1997.

For those interviews which were taped, citation is by tape number, side and minutes/seconds in brackets, e.g.: (Tape 1, B, 9.00). Some interviews were recorded by notes only and the references are to the paragraph number of the record of interview notes in brackets, e.g.: Victor Gow, 30 October 1997 (5). Transcripts of all interviews were checked with the interviewees for errors or clarification. Tapes and transcripts made of interviews will be deposited in a suitable oral history archive to be arranged. [They remain in my storage locker]

APPENDIX III

Administrative files of the Immigration (Restriction) Act

A. Nature and origins of individual files

From 1902 until 1956, immigration in Australia was carried out under the Immigration Restriction Act.[*] From 1902 until 1947 the Custom & Excise Offices of each State had responsibility for administering the Act under the direction of a variety of Commonwealth Departments.[♦] In 1947 the Department of Immigration was formed and responsibility for immigration at all levels was taken over by that Department.

In the National Archives of Australia, the files relating to individuals created by the administration of the Immigration Restriction Act are contained in two main series. The first is the C/- series or correspondence series, SP42/1. Each new application or file was given a 'C' for correspondence, followed by the year date, followed by a consecutive number. For example, the NAA: SP42/1; C33/6496, Mew Get, is a file created in 1933 for Mew Get and was the 6,496[th] file or item of correspondence of that year. As people

---

[*] In 1912 it was amended to become the Immigration Act.

[♦] These were the Department of External Affairs 1903-1916, Department of Home and Territories 1916-1928, Department of Home Affairs 1928-1932, Department of the Interior 1932-1947.

made subsequent applications or other contact with Customs, their previous files were removed and added to the new file, often called 'top numbering'. Thus, Mew Get's 1933 file also contains his applications in previous years. The NAA series SP42/1 therefore consists of all such files in chronological order of their creation.

When the Immigration Department was formed in 1947-8, the filing notation was changed, these files are in the series, SP1122/1. In NSW the 'C' was replaced by 'N' for NSW. For example, NAA: SP1122/1; N53/24/2504, Lee Man Dick (Man Duck), is a file created in 1953, the /24/ being a reference to the category 'Asiatics'. The series SP1122/1 is a continuation of SP42/1 and Lee Man Dick's file contains similar material. His file ended because he returned permanently to China while many similar files end when they do because a person became naturalised. This feature has led many researchers to refer to such files as 'naturalisation' files.

The files of these two series, SP42/1 and SP1122/1 are most fruitful because they contain the applications every person who applied for a CEDT had to provide. These applications contain at least the following information:

- *Name* (Chinese characters also given approximately 50% of the time)
- *Date of birth* (usually a year only)*
- *Date of arrival in Australia* (usually a year only)
- *Number of trips out of Australia* (length of time in China, departure/arrival dates)
- *Family* (wife and children, this question was not asked between 1905 and 1930)
- *Occupation* (past occupations, including often pre-Federation jobs)
- *Location* (past locations in Australia are listed, including those before Federation)
- *File number* (this can be used to relate the file to other material)
- *Photo* (often on the file, and always on the CEDT copy in series, ST84/1).

A typical example of such as file is: NAA: SP1122/1; N52/24/3951, John Louis (Louie) Hoon

This file consists of a series of applications for Certificates of Exemption from the Dictation Test, between 1916 and 1950, including associated Police reports, photos at various ages, hand and thumb prints, name in Chinese characters, references as to character, departmental memos and handwritten comments. Included is a police report giving a summary history of John Louie Hoon's father, Louie Hoon, dating back to his arrival in Australia in 1884. The file creates a picture of a pattern of existence for John Louie Hoon that involved extended periods of time living in both

---

* Place if given is almost invariably 'Canton.' See Appendix V.

Sydney and China. This included the presence of a wife and at least two sons in the village of Shekki (Shiqi), Zhongshan, Guangdong, China. Other information includes, occupations, addresses, and general physical description.

Chronology:

- Born 26th June, 1908 in Sydney. Described as 'half-caste', his mother 'deserting' when he was 7 years old.
- Travelled to China in March 1916 aged 7, accompanied by his father who plans to send him to 'college'.
- Returns to Sydney 19/11/24 aged 16. A note states his father, 'died 3 years ago'.
- Trip to China 9/3/28, returned 24/12/28
- Trip to China 4/3/37, returned 1939
- Trip to China 4/3/40, returned 25/10/46
- Trip to China 23/8/48, returned 18/9/50
- The final file entry is in 1955 when John Louie Hoon is working as a market gardener.

In all John Louie Hoon spent 19 years in China and 29 years in Sydney up till age 47. His file ends at this point because John Louie Hoon ceased to have any dealings with immigration officials as he never travelled again nor did he become naturalised. He continued to live in Sydney, dying there in 1987 aged 79.

B. Examples of other types of administrative files

In addition to the two large series of individual files there are many general files of interest. The NAA title of each series used in this history is given in the bibliography, however as these titles are not always accurate and can be misleading as to what each series actually contains the titles used here are more descriptive.

CEDT copies (ST84/1)

This contains a copy of every CEDT and Certificate of Domicile issued by Sydney Customs throughout the life of the Act. Each of these certificates also contains a photo of the applicant.

Copies of outward letters re: Immigration Act 1904-8, vol.1-vol.3 (A1026)

This material does not appear to have been researched previously. Examples include, letters of applications, queries concerning the operation of the Act and a report on the possible fall in Chinese numbers in Sydney gauged by comparing the imports of Chinese goods over a period and a detailed report on smuggling methods.

Register of Certificates of Exemption from the Dictation Test (SP726/1)

In six volumes this is a record of every 'Certificate of Exemption From Dictation Test' issued in NSW from 1902 to 1952. Each volume is indexed by the name of the applicant alphabetically and a record of date of arrival and departure, ship name and CEDT No. is given.

Certificates of Exemption under the Influx of Chinese Restriction Act 1881 (SP115/10)

This is a collection of certificates issued to Chinese residents of NSW granting them exemption from the 'Chinese Restriction Act of 1881'. It also includes two certificates and some receipts issued under the 1861 Act. These certificates not only reveal the administrative ancestry of the Federation Act of 1901 but also the similarity in Chinese responses to such laws in the use of agents, as revealed by the notations in Chinese on the back of many of the certificates.

General Correspondence (SP11/26)

This is a seemingly random collection of very early correspondence relating to the Immigration Act of 1901, such as petitions requesting exemption from the NSW £100 poll tax and letters requesting the picking up of CEDTs.

Certificates of Exemption by ship (SP11/6)

These files contain the records of inspection of Chinese passengers as they disembarked from various ships in Sydney in 1927-29. The individual records usually contain a 'Form 32' stating they have been identified and permitted to enter, thumb and hand prints and the returned copy of the CEDT that would have been carried on the journey. Occasional documents include a Birth Certificate with details of trips on the back, or letters from the Collector of Customs giving permission to enter Australia that were forwarded to Hong Kong.

Register of Birth Certificates (SP726/2)

This is a register kept of the Birth Certificate details of people of Chinese origin born in Australia who travelled outside Australia. There is an alphabetical index at the front with the entries by date. Most of the entries were made on people's return to Australia. Occasional remarks were made such as, 'Charlie Hoy Kee Lee/born in Sydney 1 May 1891/left when 10 months old with parents/returned 31 October 1913/Father died in China, mother in China and brother George.' The majority of entries, however, contain only basic details of dates.

Survey of aliens by Police district, 1939 (SP11/25)

In 1939, each police district in the Metropolitan area was required to count all aliens, including Chinese residing within their districts. The returns are by nationality, age and sex.

C. Brief description of Immigration Restriction Act procedures

In order to travel to the village, the Immigration Restriction Act required of the *huaqiao* that they apply for a CEDT (from 1902-7 a Certificate of Domicile). The application required various details: six photos, a thumb print (originally a full palm print), two written references as to character and a £1 fee. The police were used to verify photos, though this became less common as the *huaqiao* applied for subsequent CEDTs.

The CEDT was drawn up in duplicate and one handed to the *huaqiao* or perhaps a shipping agent by the Customs Boarding inspectors at the ship. The CEDT carried to China was necessary to purchase a ticket back to Australia. On return, the CEDT was handed in to the Boarding Inspector who compared the photos and thumbprints.

If a CEDT expired or was lost, a letter could be sent stating that the *huaqiao* would be admitted on being satisfactorily identified. On return with such a letter, a blank CEDT would be issued retrospectively.

For those who were not 'domiciles', a 'Certificate of Exemption' was issued instead. These certificates did not have photos and the category and period of validity were simply written in. On expiration, they were returned and a fresh one issued.

CEDTs in the archives.
Thousands of personal stories generated by discriminatory legislation and now a rich source of information.

APPENDIX IV
Tables of statistics and sampling methods

Table 1: Chinese populations of Australia, NSW and Sydney, 1861-1947

Year	Australia Male	Female	Total	NSW Male	Female	Total	Sydney Male	Female	Total	Year
1856				1,800	6	1,806				1856
1861			40,000	12,986	2	12,988			189	1861
1871			28,662	7,208	12	7,220			336	1871
1881	38,274	259	38,533	10,141	64	10,205			2,232	1881
1891	35,523	298	35,821	13,048	109	13,157			3,499	1891
1901	29,153	265	29,418	10,063	159	10,222			3,474	1901
1911	21,856	897	22,753	7,942	284	8,226	3,183	151	3,334	1911
1921	15,940	1,143	17,083	6,903	379	7,282	2,813	85	2,889	1921
1933	9,311	1,535	10,846	3,472	193	3,665	1,761	130	1,891	1933
1947	6,594	2,550	9,144	2,548	724	3,272	1,726	611	2,337	1947

Table 2: Percentage of Chinese in NSW and in Sydney

Year	NSW of Australia	Sydney of NSW	Sydney of Australia
1861	32.5	1.5	0.5
1871	25.2	4.6	1.1
1881	26.5	21.8	5.8
1891	36.7	26.6	9.8
1901	34.7	34.0	11.8
1911	36.2	40.5	14.6
1921	42.6	39.6	16.9
1933	33.8	51.5	17.4
1947	35.8	71.4	25.5

Tables 1 and 2 are derived from a variety of sources, most of which are ultimately derived from either Commonwealth or NSW Census data.[321] The figures are sometimes difficult to interpret, as it is not always clear when figures include both China and Australian-born people. Generally, aggregate figures are used, as the earlier data does not make

143

the distinction. 'Sydney' is also difficult to define but the general trend of the figures is clear.

CEDT derived statistics: Tables 3 to 9: Statistics for these tables are derived from the CEDT applications found on the individual files in NAA: SP42/1 and SP1122/1. A total of 130 files were examined on a random basis from the years spread across the period. These were 1903, 1911, 1913, 1920, 1929, 1931, 1933, 1936, 1941, 1946, 1947, 1952 and 1955. The details of name, date of birth, arrival, trips, family, occupation, and location were recorded and analysed to provide the statistics. As explained in Appendix III, 'top numbering' means that files in one year contain information about previous years. Files from the 1930s were generally the most fruitful, while files of the 1940s and 1950s contain more information but due to the rapid drop in *huaqiao* trips after the late 1930s there are far fewer of these files.

Table 3: Locations & Table 4: Occupations are derived from the applications for CEDTs which requested details of all previous jobs and locations. The details from the 130 files sampled were tallied to provide the distribution of both locations and occupations. As many people had multiple jobs and locations, the totals exceed 130.

Table 3: Locations

NSW location	huaqiao	per	Sydney	huaqiao	per
Sydney	98	48%	Botany	15	21%
Far West	31	15%	Nth Sydney	14	20%
Northern NSW	23	11%	Double Bay	6	9%
Queensland	11	5%	Rose Bay	5	7%
Newcastle	10	5%	Fairfield	5	7%
Brisbane	9	4%	Liverpool	5	7%
Melbourne	8	4%	Alexandria	4	6%
Victoria	4	2%	Camden	4	6%
Riverina	3	1%	Manly	3	4%
Snowy Mts	2	1%	Canterbury	2	3%
West Australia	2	1%	Waterloo	2	3%
Wollongong	1	0%	Parramatta	2	3%
South Australia	1	0%	Windsor	2	3%
			Granville	1	1%
Total	203	100%	**Total**	70	100%

Table 4: Occupations

Occupation	huaqiao	percentage	Occupation	huaqiao	percentage
Gardener	101	46%	Scrub cutter	7	3%
Labourer	23	11%	Tobacco	5	2%
Storekeeper	14	6%	Drapery	2	1%
Hawker	13	6%	Bookkeeper	2	1%
Groceries	12	5%	Farmer	2	1%
Cook	11	5%	Station work	1	0%
Cabinet Maker	11	5%	**Total**	219	100%
Carpenter	8	4%			
Miner	7	3%	Mulitple jobs	45	

145

Table 5: *Huaqiao* ages

Both the date of birth and the date of arrival in Australia were recorded, so it was a simple matter of calculating the age on arrival of each person from the sample files.

Age	huaqiao	percentage	Age	huaqiao	percentage
11	1	1%	24	5	4%
12	1	1%	25	6	5%
13	0	0%	26	5	4%
14	4	3%	27	4	3%
15	3	2%	28	8	6%
16	7	6%	29	3	2%
17	7	6%	30	3	2%
18	9	7%	31	0	0%
19	11	9%	32	2	2%
20	20	16%	33	2	2%
21	5	4%	34	1	1%
22	8	6%	35	1	1%
23	10	8%	**Total**	126	100%

Table 6: Length of time before first return

Each file began with the first application for a CEDT and this date could be used to calculate the number of years since arrival in Australia. The number of previous trips was also asked and this occasionally revealed *huaqiao* who had travelled before 1901, but this was rare.

Years	huaqiao	percentage	Years	huaqiao	percentage
4	1	1%	27	1	1%
5	0	0%	28	0	0%
6	1	1%	29	3	2%
7	1	1%	30	4	3%
8	2	2%	31	5	4%
9	3	2%	32	2	2%
10	2	2%	33	0	0%
11	4	3%	34	0	0%
12	4	3%	35	0	0%
13	5	4%	36	1	1%
14	7	5%	37	0	0%
15	7	5%	38	0	0%
16	9	7%	39	0	0%
17	13	10%	40	2	2%
18	5	4%	41	1	1%
19	7	5%	42	0	0%
20	15	11%	43	0	0%
21	3	2%	44	0	0%
22	2	2%	45	0	0%
23	0	0%	46	1	1%
24	4	3%	47	0	0%
25	3	2%	48	0	0%
26	12	9%	49	1	1%
27	1	1%	Total	131	100%

Table 7: Marriage after first sojourn

	1902-1905		1931		
No Family	15	75%	3	10%	
Wife only	3	15%	4	13%	
Widower	0	0%	1	3%	
Wife & Children	2	10%	23	74%	
Total	20	100%	31	100%	

As explained in Chapter 1, the question about family only appears between 1902-05 and again after 1930. Files were examined from both periods, including some that had information from both periods. While the sample is small, the statistics clearly shows the tendency to marry after the first sojourn to the home village, or to travel when ready to marry.

Table 8: Dates of *huaqiao* arrivals

Date of arrival in Australia was always recorded and easily tallied. Note the rises in arrivals just before new anti-Chinese migration legislation was introduced.

Year	huaqiao	percentage	Year	huaqiao	percentage
1877	3	2%	1890	4	3%
1878	0	0%	1891	5	4%
1879	0	0%	1892	7	5%
1880	2	2%	1893	6	5%
1881	2	2%	1894	6	5%
1882	0	0%	1895	9	7%
1883	5	4%	1896	9	7%
1884	4	3%	1897	11	8%
1885	4	3%	1898	10	8%
1886	7	5%	1899	7	5%
1887	16	12%	1900	3	2%
1888	4	3%	1901	1	1%
1889	6	5%	**Total**	131	100%

Table 9: Average periods spent in China

The number of previous trips and the dates of Sydney arrival and departure were all recorded on each subsequent CEDT application, this allowed the approximate length of time both in China and between sojourns to be calculated.

Time in China			Time in Australia		
Less than 12 months	23	14%	1 year	9	6%
1 year	63	39%	2 years	24	17%
2 years	43	27%	3 years	27	19%
3 years	22	14%	4 years	25	17%
4 years	4	2%	5 years	16	11%
5 years	3	2%	6 years	15	10%
6 years	1	1%	7 years	7	5%
7 years		0%	8 years	3	2%
8 years	2	1%	9 years	3	2%
9 years		0%	10 years	4	3%
			11 years	3	2%
			12 years	1	1%
			13 years	3	2%
			14 years	1	1%
			15 years	2	1%
			16 years	1	1%
Total	161	100%	**Total**	143	100%

Table 10: CEDT figures on number of trips

These statistics are taken from the Registers of CEDTs found in NAA: SP726/1. There are six volumes of registers which record for each *huaqiao* who departed Sydney the name, date of departure and arrival, ship name and CEDT number. If a person did not return then the appropriate space was left blank. 'Returns', even after many years, were back filled.

Year	Departures	Non returns	% of non returns	Year	Departures	Non returns	% of non returns
1902	72	33	46%	1931	345	132	38%
1903	274	26	9%	1932	378	83	22%
1904	290	30	10%	1933	378	100	26%
1905	354	35	10%	1934	377	81	21%
1906	439	35	8%	1935	393	80	20%
1907	594	63	11%	1936	410	104	25%
1908	725	81	11%	1937	360	101	28%
1909	787	93	12%	1938	323	100	31%
1910	750	70	9%	1939	295	110	37%
1911	860	76	9%	1940	232	118	51%
1912	1040	112	11%	1941	223	132	59%
1913	1115	104	9%	1942	0	0	0%
1914	1070	128	12%	1943	0	0	0%
1915	1137	160	14%	1944	0	0	0%
1916	986	124	13%	1945	0	0	0%
1917	738	125	17%	1946	382	115	30%
1918	662	109	16%	1947	253	103	41%
1919	862	161	19%	1948	75	30	40%
1920	867	96	11%	1949	51	20	39%
1921	1153	150	13%	1950	77	0	0%
1922	875	117	13%	1951	48	0	0%
1923	994	152	15%	1952	10	0	0%
1924	981	166	17%	1953	6	3	50%
1925	763	112	15%	1954	3	1	33%
1926	1082	217	20%	1955	12	5	42%
1927	1052	155	15%	1956	20	12	60%
1928	940	193	21%	1957	51	38	75%
1929	801	228	28%	1958	13	12	92%
1930	674	250	37%	1959	2	2	100%
1931	345	132	38%	**Total**	**27654**	**4883**	**18%**

Table 11:
Chinese passengers travelling from Sydney, 1929

These figures are based on the lists of passengers departing Sydney found in NAA: SP1148/2; Passenger lists, Outward 1929. The 'race' or 'nationality' of each passenger was always recorded and passengers transhipping from New Zealand clearly identified.

Ship	2nd class			Steerage	Totals
	Males	Females	Children		
Tanda (12/1)	18	3	6	85	106
Changte (16/1)	12	4	6	0	16
Taiping (16/2)	6	1	3	82	89
Changte (20/3)	4	0	0	72	76
Arafura (26/3)	0	0	0	19	19
Tanda (13/4)	17	2	5	53	72
Taiping (17/4)	5	0	1	22	27
Changte (22/5)	11	1	0	51	63
Arafura (15/6)	0	0	0	23	23
Taiping (19/6)	15	2	2	45	62
Tanda (13/7)	4	0	0	53	57
Changte (24/7)	8	1	5	15	24
Taiping (21/8)	4	0	1	51	55
Arafura (14/9)	0	0	0	13	13
Changte (18/9)	6	1	0	33	40
Taiping (19/10)	4	1	1	15	20
Tanda (12/10)	6	0	0	52	58
Changte (20/11)	4	0	0	46	50
St Albans (16/11)	5	1	2	3	9
Nellore (14/12)	1	2	0	38	41
Taiping (18/12)	11	1	1	24	36
Totals	**141**	**20**	**33**	**795**	**956**
	15%	2%	3%	83%	100%

Table 12: Burials and Returns

The statistics in this table are derived from the Rookwood Cemetery, Register of Burials in the 'Chinese Section of General Cemetery'. Each burial was recorded and then crossed out in red ink when exhumed. If a burial subsequently took place in the same plot it was recorded by

Year	Burials	Returned		Year	Burials	Returned	
1875	13	7	54%	1914	44	34	77%
1876	11	7	64%	1915	54	38	70%
1877	8	6	75%	1916	50	33	66%
1878	17	10	59%	1917	39	23	59%
1879	17	12	71%	1918	37	28	76%
1880	21	12	57%	1919	76	45	59%
1881	28	23	82%	1920	56	33	59%
1882	18	16	89%	1921	49	31	63%
1883	16	9	56%	1922	40	21	53%
1884	24	16	67%	1923	42	22	52%
1885	23	17	74%	1924	58	31	53%
1886	29	21	72%	1925	38	18	47%
1887	45	36	80%	1926	38	17	45%
1888	46	36	78%	1927	54	14	26%
1889	38	31	82%	1927	41	19	46%
1890	44	37	84%	1928	41	19	46%
1891	56	39	70%	1929	48	26	54%
1892	33	30	91%	1930	44	18	41%
1893	33	24	73%	1931	25	9	36%
1894	43	33	77%	1932	31	19	61%
1895	35	32	91%	1933	38	26	68%
1896	31	30	97%	1934	25	15	60%
1897	38	27	71%	1935	36	18	50%
1898	38	22	58%	1936	37	20	54%
1899	41	29	71%	1937	42	18	43%
1900	52	33	63%	1938	33	7	21%
1901	52	32	62%	1939	42	10	24%
1902	39	23	59%	1940	39		
1903	50	19	38%	1941	42		
1904	55	21	38%	1942	60		
1905	46	28	61%	1943	66		
1906	69	33	48%	1944	47		
1907	39	21	54%	1945	62		
1908	53	30	57%	1946	47		
1909	42	27	64%	1947	40		
1910	19	15	79%	1948	36	1	
1911	43	32	74%	1949	57		
1912	54	3	6%	1950	38		
1913	43	31	72%	**Total**	3094	1523	49%

being written over the same space. The figures for 'Removed' relate to the year of burial not the year of removal. Exhumations usually took place several years later.

Table 13: Arrivals in Australia by CEDTs and Certificates of Exemptions (C of E)

This information is extracted from that provided in Barry York, *Admitted: 1901 to 1946. Immigrants and others allowed into Australia between 1901 and 1946.* Centre for Immigration & Multicultural Studies, Australian National University, Canberra, 1993.

Year	CEDT	C of E	Year	CEDT	C of E
1902	121	8	1924	1544	100
1903	308	14	1925		
1904	603	31	1926	1549	99
1905	1,200	31	1927	1518	100
1906			1928	1440	118
1907	1,312	60	1929	1213	104
1908	1,628	71	1930	1025	85
1909	1,618	56	1931	665	106
1910	1,684	58	1932	562	100
1911	1,851	74	1933	444	91
1912	2,098	79	1934	490	111
1913	2,187	32	1935	460	170
1914	1,681	59	1936	461	198
1915	2,178	36	1937	470	191
1916	2,191	58	1938	426	300
1917	1,889	40	1939	293	251
1918	1,575	88	1940	187	264
1919	1,336	68	1941	148	340
1920	1,395	174	1942	0	328
1921	1,464	108	1943	0	734
1922	1,681	75	1944	0	483
1923	1,668	102	1945	0	488
			1946	8	296
			Total	44571	6379

APPENDIX V
District proportions in Sydney

An estimate of the proportions in which *huaqiao* emigrated to Australia from the various Pearl River Delta districts would be of great value in beginning the process of 'disaggregation' of the Australian-Chinese communities referred to by Henry Chan. This is of particular importance for Sydney, as it appears to have attracted an unusually wide range of districts compared to other Australian regions, particularly when compared to Melbourne's domination by the Sze Yap.[322]

The most ambitious attempt at estimating Sydney's Chinese population by district of origin was that by Dr Charles Price.[323] His findings were Chungshan (Zhongshan) - 40%, Kao Yao (Gao Yao) - 24%, Tongkoon (Dong Guan) - 20%, Sze Yap (Si Yi) - 10%, Sam Yap (San Yi) - 3% and non-Cantonese - 2%. However, these figures were based on Department of Immigration files of the late 1960s and early 70s and it cannot be assumed that the proportions had remained the same since the nineteenth century.

A Chinese Chamber of Commerce membership list of 1913 provides some comparative evidence. This membership list shows the stores and the district of origin of each manager who were members of the Chamber.[324] The table below shows the tally.

Xiangshan (Zhongshan)	香山 (中山)	6
Gao Yao	高有	4
Dong Guan	東莞	9
Xing Ning (Taishan, one of the Si Yi)	新寧 (台山)	2
He Shan (one of the San Yi)	鶴山	1
Zeng Cheng	增城	7

The most obvious difference between the estimates of Dr Price and the Chamber list is the appearance of Zeng Cheng. This is a district often associated with Dong Goon and which according to evidence given in the Royal Commission co-operated in the Loong Yee Tong.[325] The relatively few representatives of the Sze Yap districts and the preponderance of Zhongshan and Dong Guan/Zeng Cheng districts does, however, roughly fit with the Price calculations.

Of course, stores and managers do not necessarily correspond neatly with population numbers. Particularly when is possible that a manager was not from the same district as the store's orientation. This appears to have been the case with Wing On & Co., an undoubtedly Zhongshan store, whose Chamber of Commerce member was from Dong Guan.

Various estimates of society membership are also given in the Royal Commission into Alleged Chinese Gambling. At a time when the census reported the total NSW Chinese population at 13,048 and Sydney's share as 3,499, the Koon Yee Tong of the Dong Guan district is reported to have had 600 'scattered' members.[326] The Loong Yee Tong which also had Dong Guan members, as well as Zeng Cheng district members, is said to have had 1,500 members representing 80% to 90% of the community.[327] The Gao Yao are reported to have 1,000 of the 'clan' in Sydney and of the Sze Yap there were 300 in Sydney.[328]

Taking this evidence at face value and assuming all but the Koon Yee Tong evidence were referring only to Sydney, the total mentioned are 2,800. This leaves a further 700 to be made up by Zhongshan district members. This calculation would show a much higher representation for the Dong Guan and Zeng Cheng districts in the nineteenth century and a smaller one for Zhongshan than the 1970s Price estimates. Yet Zhongshan had at least two societies in operation at this time. If, however, the 1,500 for the Loong Yee Tong is taken to mean NSW and this is added to the 600 Koon Yee Tong members then the total NSW proportion for the Dong Guan and Zeng Cheng districts is not too far off the 2,600 the Price calculations would give them. The figure for the Gao Yao people in Sydney is also not too far off its Price level of about 1,000, though the Sze Yap level is twice as high.

Little definite can be said from such calculations except that it is highly likely some districts shrank in size more rapidly than others in the years between the 1891 Royal Commission and the final 'non-European' files of the Department of Immigration of the early 1970s. If further sources of figures can be found it may be possible to come to more conclusive findings.

Canton

A final confusion of identification exists over *huaqiao* places of origin. *Huaqiao* in nearly all the files and records of the Immigration Restriction Act administration give 'Canton' most often as their place of origin.[329] Officials generally were not interested in village or even district names, however, the *huaqiao* were not naming the only city in south China they thought these officials may have heard of, rather they were referring to their province of origin, Guangdong.

The Royal Commission minutes has numerous instances of witnesses replying 'Canton' when asked where they come from. Only Sun War Hop answers, 'I come from the big city in Canton.' [330] In English-speaking terms this means he actually came from the city Canton (Guangzhou). Char, op. cit., p.88, n.2, confirms this, 'When Chinese speak of themselves as being from Canton, they may mean from the province of Kwangtung [Guangdong] and not necessarily from the city of Canton. The word Canton is used instead of Kwangtungese.'

APPENDIX VI
Research in the 21ˢᵗ century✦

In the more than 25 years since the original research was done for this work a great deal of new research has naturally been done that has added much of value to our understanding of Chinese Australian history. Despite this, there remains a number of areas where more could be done. Surprisingly little for example has been done on the continuing relations and links with the villages apart from my follow up work *Returning Home with Glory*. The wonderful *South Flows the Pearl* by Mavis Yen has been mentioned in this context and mention should also be made of *Heritage and History in the China-Australia Migration Corridor* which includes work on donations to schools in the villages.

Another glaring gap is that there is still no general overview history of Chinese in Australia. This lack is perhaps related to the continuing failure of, for lack of a better term, "mainstream Australian history" to integrate or make more than token recognition (goldminers, market gardeners and Quong Tart) of the role of Chinese people in Australian history. The result is that much of the excellent work mentioned below remains in the form of a history labelled

---

✦ See end of this Appendix for these recent references.

"Chinese Australian" that runs parallel to, but only randomly intersects with, that known as "Australian history".

In addition to this inability to accept the long and deep role of Chinese people in post-contact Australian history comes the rise in the last quarter century of two new social features that have served to reenforce the old 'Chinese as victims' narratives. These are the rise of white guilt and the perspectives of new generations of people of Chinese heritage who often see the pre-1949 Chinese Australian history as their long-suffering pioneer generations. Both these perspectives have an instinctive preference to minimise agency and emphasis white racism to the detriment of nuanced history and the integration of this history into the mainstream. As might be expected such perspectives have not generated any work worth mentioning here except as work to be ignored, which is what I will do.

These negative perspectives aside, a great deal of positive history has been written that is gradually providing the foundation for a broader view of Australian history. This begins with a recognition of the role of the Amoy labourers, the 3,000 or so men brought as indentured labourers via the port of Amoy (Xiamen) many of who integrated, intermarried and contributed a great deal to 19th century

161

Australia. The work of Darnell and Slocomb are outstanding in this as are numerous family historians in demonstrating that the idea the majority of these men were worked to death in some manner, despite numerous instances of strongly resisted unfairness, is entirely false.[*]

The lack of information about Chinese women or women associated with this history is another area that many have striven to amend. The works of Bagnall and Robb are most noteworthy. Both focus on women in Australia but it should be noted that most women who played a role in this history were located in the villages of South China. My article "Holding Up Half the Family" discusses this but again more needs to be done.

More also needs to be done in specific areas where Chinese people either worked or contributed in ways that run counter to the mainstream narrative. Chinese Opera and tobacco farming are just two of interest. My "Smoking opium, puffing cigars, and drinking gingerbeer" discusses Chinese Opera how widespread was at one stage but little has been done for the also numerous Chinese tobacco growers. Flowers on Chinese medicine and Skene's work on the

---

[*] Two objects in 88 Objects are worth looking at in this context. See No.59 and No.67 at https://chinozhistory.org

Chinese contribution to football are both worth a look in this regard also.

Business is an area that has received a fair amount of attention such as Wilton and Yen Ching-hwang and most recently Fong has made another regional contribution. However, these still have not done more that scratch the surface of the complex interlinking of business and family connections both in Australia and internationally that are still to be researched. Kuo has made the best contribution to this thus far.

Another area that needs more investigation is that of politics, both in Australia and China. Fitzgerald's contribution was outstanding but no one has followed up on this lead. This is partly due to the need for much great reading of Chinese language newspapers as well as sources in China. Both avenues require Chinese languages skills (Cantonese not Mandarin and traditional characters not simplified), the lack of which hampers new research in this as in so many other areas. The translation of *The Poison of Polygamy* – a politically motivated novel – is worth mentioning in this regard.

Specific work has been done in traditional occupations such as market gardening by Boileau and furniture making by Gibson, but again so much more remains to be done.

Finally, the remittances, the sending of which was the glue that held things together rover many generations have been scarcely touched upon. The excellent work by Benton and Liu, while it mentions Australia only rarely, provides a much needed context to this significant aspect or the history.

21st Century references (mostly)

Kate Bagnall, 'Rewriting the history of Chinese families in nineteenth-century Australia', *Australian Historical Studies*, vol. 42, no. 1, March 2011: pp.62–77.

Joanna Boileau, Chinese Market Gardening in Australia and New Zealand. Gardens of Prosperity, (Palgrave, 2017).

Gregor Benton, "Australia", pp.72-91 in *Chinese Migrants and Internationalism: Forgotten Histories, 1917–1945* (Rutledge, 2007).

Gregor Benton and Hong Liu, Dear China: Emigrant Letters and Remittances, (University of California, 2018).

Denis Byrne, Ien Ang, and Phillip Mar (Eds), *Heritage and History in the China-Australia Migration Corridor*, (HKU Press, 2023).

Maxine Darnell, The Chinese labour trade to New South Wales 1783-1853: An exposition of motives and outcomes, PhD thesis, UNE, 1997.

Maxine Darnell, "Responses and Reactions to the Importation of Indentured Chinese Labourers", No. 99-2 – November 1999, *Working Paper Series in Economic History*.

Sheng Fei, "Environmental Experiences of Chinese People in the Mid-Nineteenth Century Australian Gold Rushes," *Global Environment*, 2011, 7/8: 111.

John Fitzgerald, *Big White Lie,* Sydney: UNSW Press, 2007.

James Flowers, "Chinese-Medicine Doctors Healing Australians: On the Frontline of Healthcare from the Colonial Period to the Twenty-First Century", *Translocal Chinese: East Asian Perspectives, Special Issue: The Question of Chineseness in Colonial and Postcolonial Diasporas*, Volume 16, Issue 1, 2020.

Natalie Fong, The Significance of the Northern Territory in the Formulation of 'White Australia' Policies, 1880–1901, *Australian Historical Studies*, 49:4, 2018, pp.527-545.

Peter Gibson, *Made in Chinatown: Chinese Australian Furniture Factories, 1880-1930,* Sydney University Press, 2022.

Mei-fen Kuo, *Making Chinese Australia: Urban Elites, Newspapers and the Formation of Chinese Australian Identity, 1892–1912* (Clayton, Victoria: Monash University Publishing 2013).

Juanita Kwok, *The Chinese in Bathurst: Recovering Forgotten Histories*, Doctoral thesis, Charles Sturt University, Bathurst, 2018.

Barry McGowan, "The Economics and Organisation of Chinese Mining in Colonial Australia", *Australian Economic History Review*, 2005, 45: pp.119-138.

Sandi Robb, North Queensland's Chinese family landscape: 1860-1920. PhD Thesis, James Cook University. 2019.

Patrick Skene, *Celestial Footy: the Story of Chinese Heritage Aussie Rules,* Hardie Grant Media, 2023.

Margaret Slocomb, *Among Australia's pioneers: Chinese indentured pastoral workers on the Northern Frontier 1848 to c.1880*, Bloomington, Balboa press, 2014.

Michael Williams, *Returning Home with Glory: Chinese Villagers around the Pacific, 1849 to 1949* (Hong Kong: Hong Kong University Press, 2018).

Michael Williams, Smoking opium, puffing cigars, and drinking gingerbeer: Chinese Opera in Australia, In *Opera, Emotion, and the Antipodes Volume II Applied Perspectives: Compositions and Performances*, edited by Jane W. Davidson, Michael Halliwell and Stephanie Rocke, pp.166-208. Abingdon: Routledge, 2020.

Michael Williams, Holding Up Half the Family, *Journal of Chinese Overseas* 17.1, 2021, pp.179-195.

Sophie Loy-Wilson, Coolie Alibis: Seizing Gold from Chinese Miners in New South Wales, *International Labor and Working-Class History*, 2017, Vol.91, pp.28-45.

Janis Wilton, *Golden Threads: The Chinese in Regional NSW 1850-1950,* Powerhouse Publishing, Sydney, 2004.

Wong Shee Ping, (Ely Finch, trans), *The Poison of Polygamy - A Social Novel*, University of Sydney Press, 2019.

Yen Ching-hwang, "Wing On and the Kwok Brothers: a case study of pre-war Chinese entrepreneurs" in Kerrie L. MacPherson, *Asian Department Stores*, Curzon, 1998, pp.34-47.

Mavis Yen, (Siaoman Yen & Richard Horsburgh, eds), *South Flows the Pearl,* (Sydney University Press, 2022).

Special Note: Publications of Morag Jeanette Loh (nee Foster)

Not only was Morag Loh ahead of her times in doing this excellent research but her pre-digital and non-academic choice of publications means that much of her work is difficult to access now. This is a great pity and I plan to publish a collection of her work.

Loh, Morag, John Egge: a champion of the rivers, *Hemisphere*, 28 (1), 1983, pp.35-39.

Loh, Morag, 'You're my diamond, mum!': Some thoughts on women married to immigrants from China in Victoria from the 1850s to the 1920, *Oral History Association of Australia Journal*, 1984, Issue 6, p.3-10.

Loh, Morag, 'Victoria and a catalyst for Western and Chinese Medicine', *RHSV Journal* 1985, 56(3):38-46.

Loh, Morag and Grant, J., *Sojourners and settlers: Chinese in Victoria 1848-1985*, Melbourne: Victorian Government China Advisory Committee, 1985.

Loh, Morag and Ramsay, Christine, *Survival and celebration: an insight into the lives of Chinese immigrant women, European women married to Chinese and their female children in Australia from 1856 to 1986*, Melbourne: M. Loh and C. Ramsay, 1986.

Loh, Morag, "Historical overview of Chinese migration", in Hanks, Peter (ed) and Perry, Andrew (ed). *The Chinese in Australia: papers from the conference held on 19 March 1988*. Clayton, Vic: Centre for Migrant and Intercultural Studies, Monash University, 1988, p1-6. (Working Papers on Migrant and Intercultural Studies).

Loh, Morag, "Chinese-Australian true blue Diggers", *Focus*, Jun 1988, p3.

Loh, Morag, "Thomas Coto [Series of two parts] Part 1: From seafarer to successful farmer, *Gippsland Heritage Journal*, v.3, no.2, 1988: 11-14.

Loh, Morag, "Thomas Coto [Series of two parts] Part 2: Adaptable immigrant: exemplary citizen", *Gippsland Heritage Journal*, no.6, June 1989: 40-43.

Loh, Morag, "Rough road to equality: attitudes to Chinese migration 1847/ 1988", *Magazine* (Chinese Association of Victoria), 1989: 54-59.

Loh, Morag, Chinese Anzacs: the launch of Dinky-Di, *Focus for a Multicultural Australia*, n7, Oct 1989, p2.

Loh, Morag with Judith Winternitz, *Dinky Di: The Contributions Of Chinese Immigrants And Australians Of Chinese Descent To Australia's Defence Forces And War Efforts 1899-1988*, Canberra, ACT: Australian Government Publishing Service for Office of Multicultural Affairs, 1989.

Loh, Morag, "The Chinese Times 1902-1922", *La Trobe Library Journal*, Vol. 13, No. 53, Oct 1994: 12-16. [online]

Loh, Morag. "An outpost of the Chinese medical tradition: the practice of Thomas Chong, Bairnsdale", *Gippsland Heritage Journal*, no.18, June 1995: 2-7.

Morag Loh, "Fighting uphill: Australians of Chinese descent and the defence forces, 1899-1951", in Ryan, Jan (ed). *Chinese in Australia and New Zealand: a multidisciplinary approach*. New Delhi: New Age International, 1995, pp.59-66.

Morag Loh, *Grandpa and Ah Gong* (1995), with Xiangyi Mo, illustrator, South Melbourne, Vic.: Hyland House, 1995.

REFERENCES

Primary Sources

<u>Government Archives</u>

National Archives of Australia (NSW)

> SP42/1; Correspondence of the Collector of Customs relating to Immigration Restrictions and Passports, 1898-1948.

> SP1122/1; General Correspondence and Case files, 1901-1967.

> ST84/1; Certificates of Exemption From Dictation Test, 1904-1959.

> A1026; Outward letters books, Correspondence in connection with the Immigration Act 1904-8, vol.1-vol.3.

> SP726/1; Register of Certificates Exempting from the Dictation Test, 1902-1959.

> SP115/10; Certificates Exempting from the provisions of the Influx of Chinese Restrictions Act of 1881, 1862-1888.

> SP11/26; Applications for Certificates of Domicile, 1897-1910.

> SP11/6; Certificates of Exemption from the Dictation Test, 1902-1946.

> SP726/2; Register of Birth Certificates, 1902-1962.

> SP11/25; Aliens Returns for December 9th, 1939, NSW, 1939-1940.

> SP1148/2; Passenger lists, Outward 1902, 1929 & 1939.

> (See appendix III for descriptions of these National Archives of Australia files.)

National Archives of Australia (Canberra)

> A1; 1903/3081, Instructions re: Certificate of Domiciles, minute, 26 November 1902.

> A6980/T1; S250386, Non-European Policy Review 1962.

<u>Private archives and records</u>

Rookwood Cemetery, Anglican Trust: Register of Burials in the Necropolis at Haslem's Creek, under the Necropolis Act of 1867, 31st Victoria, no.14, 'Chinese Section of General Cemetery'.

Noel Butlin Archives Centre: Chinese Chamber of Commerce of NSW and other Chinese Associations Deposit 111, Australian National University.

Mar Letters. A collection of letters and sundry documents written to and from Harry Fay from c.1912 to the 1950s. Copies held by Dr Janis Wilton, University of New England.

<u>Government Reports</u>

Report of the Royal Commission on Alleged Chinese Gambling and Immorality and Charges of Bribery Against Members of the Police Force. Appointed August 20th 1891. Government Printer, Sydney, 1892.

Official Year Book of the Commonwealth of Australia, no.6, 1901-1912, Commonwealth Bureau of Census and Statistics, Melbourne, 1913.

Official Year Book of the Commonwealth of Australia, no.18, 1925, Commonwealth Bureau of Census and Statistics, Melbourne, 1925.

Official Year Book of the Commonwealth of Australia, no.28, 1935, Commonwealth Bureau of Census and Statistics, Melbourne, 1936.

Coghlan, T. A., *NSW Statistical Register for 1899 and Previous Year,* Sydney, Government Printer, 1900.

Statistical Register of New South Wales for 1886, Government Statisticians Office, Government Printer, Sydney, 1887.

NSW Statistical Register for 1919-20, NSW Government Statisticians Office, NSW Government Printer, Sydney, 1921.

Oral History interviews

- Arthur Gar-Lock Chang, Sydney, 28 October 1997.
- Cliff Lee, Sydney, 28 September 1997 and Zhongshan, January 1998.
- Victor Gow, Sydney, 30 October 1997.
- Norman Lee, Sydney, 25 September 1997.
- Donald Young, Sydney, 11 October 1997.
- Billy Gay, Sydney, 19 March 1998.
- King Fong, Sydney, 1 April 1998.

Photos

Victor Gow photos: (Courtesy of Victor Gow)
House built by Joe Wah Gow, Long Tou Wan village, Zhongshan, China. Photo taken sometime in the 1960s.

Michael Williams photos:
Lee Man Dick and his wives, photo taken with permission of Cliff Lee, January, 1998.
Anthony Hordern safe and logo, photo taken with permission of Cliff Lee, January, 1998.
Tower House, Jin Huan Village, Zhongshan, south China. Photo taken, January, 1998.
Quong Sin Tong structure, Old Chinese Section, Rookwood Cemetery, Sydney. Photo taken, March, 1998.

Newspapers & Journals

'Chinese refutation of Anti-Chinese and Asiatic League attacks', *Sydney Morning Herald*, 22 August 1904.

'Chinese in Sydney', *The Sydney Mail*, 25 February 1903.

'Chinese life in Sydney', *Illustrated Sydney News*, 12 June 1880.

'Chinese delegation to the Prime Minister', *Daily Telegraph*, 30 December 1902.

'The Belmore Markets', *Dalgety's Weekly*, 1 January 1902.

Clark, W. H., 'Our Vegetable Supply', *The Agricultural Gazette of NSW*, vol. XII, Part 12, Dec, 1901, pp.1606-1613.

Egerton, Margaret, 'My Chinese', *The Cosmos Magazine*, Sept, pp.124-128, Oct, pp.138-141, Nov, pp.192-196, 1896.

The Chinese Australian Herald, 廣益華報, 3 June 1903.

Tung Wah News, 東華新報, 9 March 1901.

Chinese Republic News, 13 September 1919 and 20 September 1919.

Chinese Repository, vol. 1, May 1832, no.1, Canton 1833, (2nd edn, Japan, n.d).

Secondary Sources

Chinese language articles

Chen Shanying 陳山鷹, "Cong qiaokan xiangxun ziliao kan: Meiguo huaqiao huaren de gutu guannian" 從僑刊鄉訊資料看美國華僑華人的故土觀念 (From overseas Chinese publications: American overseas Chinese people ideas of the homeland), *Huaqiao huaren lishi yanjiu* 華僑華人歷史研究 (Overseas Chinese History Researches), No.3, 1991, pp.1-8.

Cheng, Lucie 成露西, "Meiguo huaren yanjiu" 美國華人研究 (American Chinese Researches), *Qiaoshi xuebao* 僑史學報 (Journal of Overseas Chinese History), No.1 June 1989, pp.229-33.

Dai Yifeng 戴一峰, "Jindai Fujian huaqiao huaren chu ru guo guimo ji qi fazhan bianhua" 近代福建華僑華人出入國規模及其發展變化 (Modern Fujian Overseas Chinese in/out flows, scale and changes in development), *Huaqiao huaren lishi yanjiu* 華僑華人歷史研究 (Overseas Chinese History Researches), 2, 1988, pp.33-39.

Dong Ren 東人, " 'Zhuzai' chengwei youlai kaolue" "豬仔" 稱謂由來考略 ('Piggies' Textual research on the origin of the term), *Huaqiao huaren lishi yanjiu* 華僑華人歷史研究 (Overseas Chinese History Researches), 3, 1989, p.61.

Feng Yuan 馮元, "Luelun jiefang qian guangdongsheng huaqiao huikuan" 略論解放前廣東省 華僑滙款 (A brief discussion of Guangdong overseas Chinese remittances before liberation), *Qiaoshi xuebao* 僑史學報 (Journal of Overseas Chinese History), 1, 1989, pp.31-40.

Gao Minchuan 高民川, "Zhongshanshi huaqiao dashiji" 中山市華僑大事記 (Record of major events of Zhongshan City overseas Chinese), *Zhongshan wenshi* 中山文史 (Zhongshan Cultural History), Vol.20, 1990, pp.7-29.

Huang Chongyan 黃重言, "Yanjiu huaqiaoshi shang de jidian yijian" 研究華僑史上的幾點意見 (A few comments about researching overseas Chinese history), *Huaqiao lunwen shi* 華僑論文史 (Overseas Chinese History Thesis), No.1, April 1982, pp.24-28.

Huang Daoji 黃道記 & Liu Chongmin 劉重民, "Taishanren shewai jiaowang yu chuyang suyuan" 台山人涉外交往與出洋溯源 (The origin of Taishan people's overseas migration and their links), *Qiaoshi xuebao* 僑史學報 (Journal of Overseas Chinese History), No.1, 1989, pp.7-8.

Kan Yanxin 闞延鑫, "Cong Kaiping huaqiao bowuguan wenwu cangpin, kan huaqiao dui zuguo de gongxian" 從開平華僑博物館文物藏品, 看華僑對祖國的貢獻 (From the collection of the Kaiping Museum to see the overseas Chinese contribution to the home country), *Qiaoshi xuebao* 僑史學報 (Journal of Overseas Chinese History), 1, 1987, pp.44-49.

Lin Jinzhi 林金枝, "Cong zupu ziliao kan min yue renmin yiju haiwai de huodong ji qi dui jiaxiang de gongxian" 從族譜資料看閩粵人民移居海外的活動及其對家鄉的貢獻 (A look at clan records to see the overseas activities of Fujian and Guangdong people and their contribution to their hometowns), *Huaqiao huaren lishi yanjiu* 華僑華人歷史研究 (Overseas Chinese History Researches), 1, 1991, pp.16-23.

Miao Wenyue 繆文雨 & Gao Huanzhang 高煥章, "Shiqi yinye de huiyi" 石岐銀業的回憶 (Recollections of the Shiqi silver industry), *Zhongshan wenshi* 中山文史 (Zhongshan Cultural History), Vol.1-3, [1962-1965], 1989, pp.88-95.

Wu Fengbin 吳風斌, "Youguan qiyue huagong de jige wenti" 有關契約華工的幾個問題 (A few questions regarding Chinese Contract Workers), *Huaqiao huaren lishi yanjiu* 華僑華人歷史研究 (Overseas Chinese History Researches), 2, 1989, pp.14-21.

Xiong Yue 熊越, "Luelun jindai Xiamen de huaqiao huikuan ji qi zuoyong" 略論近代廈門的華僑匯款及其作用 (A brief discussion of Modern Xiamen's remittances and their function), *Huaqiao huaren lishi yanjiu* 華僑華人近代歷史研究 (Overseas Chinese History Researches), No.4, 1990, pp.16-21.

Zheng Dehua 鄭德華 & Wu Xingci 吳行賜, "Yipi youjiazhi de huaqiaoshi ziliao - Taishan jiefangqian chuban de zazhi, zukan pingjie" 一批有價值的華僑史資料－台山解放前出版的雜誌, 族刊評介 (A Collection of valuable overseas Chinese history information - A review of Pre-Liberation Taishan Magazines and Clan publications), *Huaqiao lunwen shi* 華僑論文史 (Overseas Chinese History Thesis), No.1, April 1982, pp.454-489.

Zheng Dehua 鄭德華, "Shijiu shiji mo Taishan qiaoxiang de xingcheng ji qi pouxi" 十九世紀末台山僑鄉的形成及其剖析 (A analysis of the formation of overseas emigrant communities in Taishan in the late 19th century), *Qiaoshi xuebao* 僑史學報 (Journal of Overseas Chinese History), No.3, 1986, pp.33-39.

Zheng Shanyu 鄭山玉, "Huaqiao yu hai shang sichou zhi lu -
bufen qiaoxiang zupu zhong de haiwai yimin ziliao fenxi" 華僑
與海上絲綢之路 – 部分僑鄉族譜中的海外移民資料分析
(Overseas Chinese and the Silk Road of the Sea - An analysis of
overseas migration information of clan records in part of the
emmigrant communities), *Huaqiao huaren lishi yanjiu* 華僑華人
歷史研究 (Overseas Chinese History Researches), No.1, 1991,
pp.23-30.

Zheng Shanyu 鄭山玉, "Luelun qiaoxiang zupu zai huaqiao lishi
yanjiu shang de ziliao jiazhi" 略論僑鄉族譜在華僑歷史研究上
的資料價值 (A brief discussion of the information value of
overseas Chinese community Clan records in overseas Chinese
historical research), *Huaqiao huaren lishi yanjiu* 華僑華人歷史
研究 (Overseas Chinese History Researches), No.1, 1991, pp.31-
34.

Zhou Xiaozhong 周孝中, "Haiwai huaqiao yu shenggong
bagong" 海外華僑與省港罷工 (Overseas Chinese abroad and a
provincial port strike), *Huaqiao lunwen shi* 華僑論文史
(Overseas Chinese History Thesis), No.1, April, 1982, p.258.

English language articles

Atkinson, Anne, 'Chinese labour in Western Australia', *Time
Remembered*, 6, 1984, pp.164-178.

Cheng, Lucie & Liu Yuzun with Zheng Dehua, 'Chinese
Emigration, the Sunning Railway and the Development of
Toisan', *Amerasia Journal*, 9/1, 1982, pp.59-74.

Chan, Anthony B., 'Orientalism' and image making: The
Sojourner in Canadian History', *The Journal of Ethnic Studies,*
9/3, 1981, pp.37-46.

Chan, Wellington K. K., 'The Organisational Structure of the
Traditional Chinese Firm and its Modern Reform', *Business
History Review,* vol. 56, Summer, 1982, pp.218-235.

Cushman, J.W., 'A 'Colonial Casualty': The Chinese community in Australian Historiography', *Asian Studies Association of Australia*, vol.7, no 3, April, 1984.

Godley, Michael R., 'The Sojourners: Returned Overseas Chinese in the People's Republic of China', *Pacific Affairs,* 6/3, 1989, pp.330-352.

Hayden, Albert A., 'NSW Immigration Policy, 1856-1900', *Transactions of the American Philosophical Society*, vol 61, Pt 5, 1971.

Hsu, Francis L. K., 'Influence of South-Seas emigration on certain Chinese Provinces', *Far Eastern Quarterly,* 5/1, 1945, pp.47-59.

Lai Chuen-yan David, 'An analysis of data on home journeys by Chinese immigrants in Canada, 1892-1915', *The Professional Geographer,* 29/4, 1977, pp.359-65.

Liu Haiming, 'The Trans-Pacific Family: A Case Study of Sam Chang's Family History', *Amerasia Journal,* 18/2, 1992, p.1-34.

Loh, Morag, 'You're My Diamond, Mum!' Some thoughts on women married to immigrants from China in Victoria from the 1860s to the 1920s', *Oral History Association of Australia Journal,* no. 6, 1984.

Markus, Andrew, 'Chinese in Australian History', *Meanjin*, 42.1, March, 1983.

Mei, June, 'Socioeconomic origins of emigration: Guangdong to California 1850-1882', *Modern China,* vol. 5, no.4, June, 1979, pp.463-501.

Nairn, N. B., 'A Survey of the History of the White Australia Policy in the Nineteenth Century', *The Australian Quarterly,* vol. XXVIII, no.3, September, 1956, pp.16-31.

Ng, Franklin, 'The Sojourner, return migration, and immigration history', *Chinese America: History and Perspectives*, 1987, pp 53-71.

Oddie, G., 'The Lower Class Chinese and the Merchant Elite in Victoria, 1870-1890', *Historical Studies,* vol.10, no.37, November, 1961, pp.65-69.

Palfreeman, A. C., 'The End of the Dictation Test', *The Australian Quarterly,* vol.XXX, no.1, March, 1957, pp.26-38.

Palfreeman, A. C., 'Some Implication of Asian Immigration', *The Australian Quarterly,* vol.XXIX, no.1, March, 1958, pp.43-50.

Peterson, Glen D., 'Socialist China and the Huaqiao. The Transition to Socialism in the Overseas Chinese Areas of Rural Guangdong, 1949-1956', *Modern China,* vol. 14, no.3, July, 1988, pp.309-335.

Sinn, Elizabeth, 'Xin Xi Guxiang: A Study of Regional Associations as a Bonding Mechanism in the Chinese Diaspora. The Hong Kong Experience', *Modern Asian Studies,* 31/2, 1997, pp.375-397.

Siu, Paul C.P., 'The Sojourner', *The American Journal of Sociology,* LVII, July, 1952, pp.34-44.

Wang Gungwu, 'South China perspective's on overseas Chinese', *The Australian Journal of Chinese Affairs,* no.13, 1984, pp.69-84.

Wang Gungwu, 'Upgrading the Migrant: Neither Huaqiao nor Huaren', *Chinese America: History and Perspectives*, 1996, pp 1-18.

Woon, Y.F., 'An Emigrant Community in the Ssu-yi Area, Southeastern China, 1885-1949: A Study in Social Change', *Modern Asian Studies*, 18/2 1984, pp.273-306.

Woon, Y.F., 'Social Change and Continuity in South China: Overseas Chinese and the Guan Lineage of Kaiping County, 1949-87', *China Quarterly,* 118, June, 1989, pp.324-344.

Woon, Y.F., 'International Links and the Socioeconomic Development of Rural China. An Emigrant Community in Guangdong', *Modern China,* vol. 16, no.2, April, 1990. pp.139-172.

Yen Ching-Hwang, 'Chang Yu-nan and the Chaochow Railway (1904-1908): A Case Study of Overseas Chinese Involvement in China's Modern Enterprise', *Modern Asian Studies*, 18/1, 1984, pp.119-135.

Yong, C. F., 'Ah Mouy Louis (1826-1918)', *Australian Dictionary of Biography*, vol.3, 1851-1890, Melbourne University Press, Victoria, 1969, p.19-20.

Yu, Elena S. H., 'Overseas remittances in South-eastern China', *China Quarterly*, 79, 1979, pp.339-350.

Yu Lan Poon, 'The two-way mirror: contemporary issues as seen through the eyes of the Chinese language press, 1901-1911', Chapter 3, pp.50-65 in Fitzgerald, Shirley & Wotherspoon, Garry (ed.) *Minorities: Cultural Diversity in Sydney,* State Library of New South Wales Press in association with the Sydney History Group, Sydney, 1995.

Yu Renqiu, 'Chinese American Contributions to the Educational Development of Toisan 1910-1940', *Amerasia Journal,* 10/1, 1983, pp.47-72.

Zo Kil Young, 'Emigrant Communities in China, Sze-Yap', *Asian Profile,* vol.5, no.4, August, 1977, pp.313-23.

Chinese language books

Chen Chih-fu 陳直夫, *Ao-chou chi lu Ao Hua Ch'iao* 澳洲與旅澳華僑 (Australia and Australian Overseas Chinese Travel), (上海：商務, 民國 36, Shanghai: Shangwu yin shu kuan, 1947)

Kaipingxian huaqiao bowuguan 開平縣華僑博物館 (Kaiping Overseas Chinese Museum, Ed.), *Kaipingxian wenwu zhi* 開平縣文物志 (Kaiping County Cultural Records), (Guangdong renmin chubanshe 廣東人民出版社 Guangdong People Publishing House, 1989)

Taishanxian qiaowu bangongshi 台山縣僑務辦公室 (Taishan County Overseas Affairs Office, Ed.), *Taishanxian huaqiao zhi* 台山縣華僑志 (Taishan County overseas Chinese Records),

(Taishanxian qiaowu bangongshi 台山縣僑務辦公室 Taishan County Overseas Affairs Office, 1992).

Zheng Jiarui 鄭嘉銳, "Xuelishi zhongshan huaqiao yiji kaocha jishi" 雪梨市中山華僑遺跡考察記事 (A record of investigations of the remains of Sydney Zhongshan overseas Chinese), *Zhongshan wenshi* 中山文史 (Zhongshan Cultural History), Vol.24, 1992, pp.40-52.

Zhongshanshi Difangzhi Bianzuan Weiyuanhui Bian 中山市地方志編纂委員會編 (Zhongshan Local records committee [Ed.]), *Zhongshanshi zhi* 中山市志 (Zhongshan City Records), (廣東: 廣東人民出版社, Guangdong Peoples Publishing Co., 1997).

English language books

Andrews, Eric Montgomery, *Australia and China: the ambiguous relationship,* Melbourne University Press, Melbourne, 1985.

Australian Dictionary of Biography, vol.1-vol.6, Melbourne University Press, Calton, 1966-1993.

Baker, Hugh, *Chinese Family & Kinship,* Macmillan Press, London, 1979.

Barth, Gunther, *Bitter Strength,* Harvard University Press, Cambridge, Massachusetts, 1964.

Brawley, Sean, *The White Peril - Foreign Relations and Asian Immigration to Australasia and North America 1919-1978,* UNSW Press, Sydney, 1995.

Campbell, Persia Crawford, *Chinese Coolie Emigration to Countries Within the British Empire,* P.S. King & Sons, Westminster, 1923.

Chang, Chung-li, *The Income of the Chinese Gentry*, University of Washington, Seattle, 1962.

Char Tin-Yuke, *The Sandalwood Mountains. Readings and Stories of the Early Chinese in Hawaii,* The University Press of Hawaii, Honolulu, 1975.

Chen Hen-Seng, *Landlord and Peasant in China – A Study of the Agrarian crisis in South China,* (International Publishers, NY, 1936), Hyperion Press, Connecticut, 1973.

Chen Ta, *Emigrant Communities in South China: A Study of Overseas Migration and its influence on standards of living and social change,* Institute of Pacific Relations, New York, 1940 (1939).

Ch'ng, David, *The Overseas Chinese Entrepreneurs in East Asia: background, business practices and international networks,* Committee for Economic Development of Australia, Sydney, 1993.

Choi, C. Y., *Chinese Migration and Settlement in Australia,* Sydney University Press, Sydney, 1975.

Cole, E. W., *Better Side of the Chinese Character*, Melbourne, 1918.

Cronin, Kathryn, *Colonial Casualties: Chinese in Early Victoria*, Melbourne University Press, Melbourne, 1982.

Cushman, Jennifer W. & Wang Gungwu (eds), *Changing Identities of the Southeast Asian Chinese Since World War II*, Hong Kong University Press, Hong Kong, 1988.

Dreyer, Edward L., *China at War 1901-1949,* Longmans, 1995.

Elegant, Robert, *The Dragon's Seed,* St Martin's Press, New York, 1959.

Faure, David & Siu, Helen (eds) *Down to Earth. The Territorial Bond in South China,* Stanford University Press, Stanford, California, 1995.

Fitzgerald, Shirley, *Red Tape, Gold Scissors,* State Library of NSW Press, Sydney, 1997.

Fitzgerald, Stephen, *China and the Overseas Chinese; a study of Peking's changing policy, 1949-1970,* Cambridge University Press, 1972.

Freedman, Maurice, *Chinese Lineage and Society: Fukien and Kwangtung,* University of London, Athlone Press, 1966.

Giese, Diana, *Beyond Chinatown: Changing Perspectives on the Top End Chinese Experience*, National Library of Australia, Canberra, 1995.

Giese, Diana, *Astronauts, Lost Souls & Dragons: voices of today's Chinese Australians*, University of Queensland Press, St Lucia, 1996.

Gittins, Jean, *The Diggers from China: The story of the Chinese on the Goldfields,* Quartet Books, Melbourne, 1981.

Godley, Michael, *The Mandarin-capitalists from Nanyang,* Cambridge University Press, 1981.
Hicks, George L. (ed.), *Overseas Chinese Remittances from Southeast Asia, 1910-1940,* Select Books, Singapore, 1993.

Ho Ping-Ti, *The Ladder of Success in Imperial China,* Colombia University Press, New York, 1967.

Hornage, Bill, *The Yellow Peril,* Review Publications, Dubbo, 1971.

Huang Tsen-ming, *The Legal Status of the Chinese Abroad: Overview of legal conditions in the US, British Empire, French and Dutch East Indies*, 2nd edition, China Cultural Service, Taipei, 1954.

Huck, Arthur, *The Chinese in Australia,* Longmans, Melbourne, 1963.

Loh, Morag Jeanette (Judith Winternitz, ed.), *Dinky-di: the contributions of Chinese immigrants and Australians of Chinese descent to Australia's defence forces and war efforts 1899-1988,* Australian Government Publishing Service, Canberra, 1989.

London, Herbert Ira, *Non-white Immigration and the White Australia Policy*, Sydney Uni Press, Sydney, 1970.

Museum of Chinese Australian History, *Histories of the Chinese in Australasia and the South Pacific,* Museum of Chinese Australian History, Melbourne,1995.

Macnair, H. F., *The Chinese Abroad Their Position and Protection. A Study in International Law and Relations,* The Commercial Press, Shanghai, 1925.

Markus, Andrew, *Fear and Hatred: purifying Australia and California, 1850-1901,* Hale & Iremonger, Sydney, 1979.

May, Cathie, *Topsawyers: the Chinese in Cairns 1870 to 1920*, James Cook University, Townsville, 1984.

Mo Yimei, *William J. Liu, O.B.E. - Pathfinder, 1893-1983,* Australia-China Chamber of Commerce and Industry of New South Wales, Canberra, 1991.

Moser, Leo J., *The Chinese Mosaic. The Peoples and Provinces of China.* Westview, London, 1985.

Palfreeman, A. C., *The Administration of the White Australia Policy,* Melbourne University Press, Melbourne, 1967.

Price, Charles Archibald, *The Great White Walls are Built: Restrictive Immigration to North America and Australasia, 1836-1888,* Australian Institute of International Affairs in association with Australian National University Press, Canberra, 1974.

Purcell, V. W., *Chinese in Southeast Asia.* Oxford University Press, 2nd Edition, 1966 (1951).

Reid, Anthony (ed.), *Sojourners and Settlers: histories of Southeast Asia and the Chinese,* Asian Studies Association of Australia in association with Allen & Unwin, Sydney, 1996.

Rhoads, J. M., *China's Republican Revolution – The Case of Kwangtung, 1895-1913,* Harvard University Press, Cambridge, Massachusetts, 1975.

Rolls, Eric, *Sojourners: flowers and the wide sea,* vol.1, University of Queensland Press, St Lucia, 1992.

Rolls, Eric, *Citizens: flowers and the wide sea,* vol.2, University of Queensland Press, St Lucia, 1996.

Ross, I. Clunies, *Australia and the Far East. History of Oriental Trade Contacts and Diplomacy,* Australian Institute of International Affairs, Angus and Robertson, 1935.

Ryan, Jan, *Ancestors: Chinese in Colonial Australia*, Fremantle Arts Centre, Fremantle, 1995.

Ryan, Jan (ed.), *Chinese in Australia and New Zealand: a multidisciplinary approach*, New Age International, New Delhi, 1995.

Saunders, Kay (ed.), *Indentured Labour in the British Empire 1834-1920*, Croom Helm, Canberra, 1984.

Sinn, Elizabeth, *Power and Charity – The Early History of the Tung Wah Hospital, Hong Kong,* Oxford University Press, Hong Kong, 1989.

Siu, Helen F., *Agents and Victims in South China – Accomplices in Rural Revolution,* Yale University Press, New Haven & London, 1989.

Somers Heidhues, Mary F., *Southeast Asia's Chinese Minorities,* Longman, Hawthorn, 1974.

Spence, Jonathan D., *The Search for Modern China,* W.W. Norton & Co., New York, 1990.

Stacker, Julie & Stewart Perri, *Chinese Immigrants and Chinese-Australians in NSW*, Guide 1, National Archives of Australia, NSW Office, August, 1996.

Stockard, Janice E., *Daughters of the Canton Delta - Marriage Patterns and Economic Strategies in South China 1860-1930*, Stanford University Press, California, 1989.

Tart, Margaret, *The Life of Quong Tart: or How a Foreigner Succeeded in a British Community*, Sydney, 1911.

Topley, Marjorie, *Marriage Resistance in Rural Kwangtung*, Stanford University Press, California, 1975.

Travers, Robert, *Australian Mandarin: the life and times of Quong Tart*, Kangaroo Press, Kenthurst, 1981.

Tweedie, Sandra M., *Trading Partners: Australia and Asia 1790-1993*, University of New South Wales Press, Sydney, 1994.

Wakeman, Frederic, *The Fall of Imperial China*, Free Press, New York, 1975.

Wang Gungwu, *China and the Chinese overseas*, Times Academic Press, Singapore, 1991.

Wang Gungwu, *Community and Nation: China, Southeast Asia, and Australia*, Asian Studies Association of Australia in association with Allen & Unwin, Sydney, 1992.

Watson, James L, *Emigration and the Chinese Lineage: the Mans in H.K. and London*, University of California Press, Berkeley, 1975.

Weber, Max, *The Religion of China*, The Macmillan Co., New York, 1964.

Willard, Myra, *History of the White Australia Policy to 1920*, 2nd edition, Melbourne University Press, Melbourne, 1967.

Williams, Michael, *Australia's Dictation Test: The Test it was a Crime to Fail*, Brill, 2021.

Wu, C.H., *Dollars Dependents and Dogma; o/seas Chinese remittances to Communist China*, The Hoover Institution on War, Revolution and Peace, Stanford, California, 1967.

Yarwood, A. T., *Asian Migration to Australia: the background to exclusion, 1896-1923*, Melbourne University Press, Melbourne, 1964.

Yen, Ching-Hwang, *Studies in Modern Overseas Chinese History*, Times Academic Press, New York, 1995.

Yong, C. F. (Ching Fatt), *The New Gold Mountain: the Chinese in Australia, 1901-1921,* Raphael Arts, Richmon, South Australia, 1977.

York, Barry, *Admitted: 1901 to 1946. Immigrants and Others Allowed into Australia between 1901 and 1946,* Centre for Immigration & Multicultural Studies, Australian National University, 1993.

York, Barry, *Admissions and Exclusions: 'Asiatics' and 'other coloured races' in Australia: 1901 to 1946,* Centre for Immigration & Multicultural Studies, Australian National University, 1995.

Young, Faye & van Barnevald, Nicole, *Sources for Chinese Local History and Heritage in New South Wales,* n.p., 1997.

Unpublished Theses

Burrage, Vivien Suit-Cheng, The Chinese community, Sydney, 1870-1901, Masters thesis, Macquarie University, 1974.

Choy Chi Cheung, Descent Group unification and segmentation in the coastal area of southern China. PhD thesis, University of Tokyo, 1987.

Darnell, Maxine, The Chinese Labour Trade to New South Wales, 1783-1853, PhD thesis, University of New England, 1997.

Wilton, Janis, Chinese Voices, Australian Lives: Oral history and the Chinese contribution to Glen Innes, Inverell, Tenterfield and surrounding districts during the first half of the twentieth century, PhD thesis, University New England, August, 1996.

Introduction

[1] Interview, Professor Zhou Muheng (周慕珩), Long Tou Wan village, Zhongshan District, Guangdong Province, China, 15 January 1998.

[2] Kan Yanxin 闞延鑫, "Cong Kaiping huaqiao bowuguan wenwu cangpin, kan huaqiao dui zuguo de gongxian" 從開平華僑博物館文物藏品, 看華僑對祖國的貢獻 (From the collection of the Kaiping Museum to see the overseas Chinese contribution to the home country), *Qiaoshi xuebao* 僑史學報 (*Journal of Overseas Chinese History*), 1, 1987, p.44.

[3] NAA: SP1122/1; N1952/24/3951, John Louis (Louie) Hoon, file note, 11 July 1955.

[4] For a brief history of this district see, Choy Chi Cheung, Descent Group unification and segmentation in the coastal area of southern China. PhD thesis, University of Tokyo, 1987, pp.69-75. Also, Char Tin-Yuke, *The Sandalwood Mountains. Readings and Stories of the Early Chinese in Hawaii,* The University Press of Hawaii, Honolulu, 1975, pp.20-23.

[5] Myra Willard, *History of the White Australia Policy to 1920*, 2nd edn, Melbourne University Press, Melbourne, 1967.

[6] A.T.Yarwood, *Asian Migration to Australia: the background to exclusion*, Melbourne University Press, Melbourne, 1964.

[7] A. C. Palfreeman, *The Administration of the White Australia Policy,* Melbourne University Press, Melbourne, 1967; Herbert Ira London, *Non-white Immigration and the 'White Australia' Policy*, Sydney University Press, Sydney, 1970; Albert A. Hayden, 'NSW Immigration Policy, 1856-1900', *Transactions of the American Philosophical Society,* 1971; Sean Brawley, *The White Peril - Foreign Relations and Asian Immigration to Australasia and North America 1919-1978,* University of New South Wales Press, Sydney, 1995.

[8] Charles Price, *The Great White Walls are Built: Restrictive Immigration to North America and Australasia, 1836-1888,* Australian Institute of International Affairs in association with Australian National University Press, Canberra, 1974; Andrew Markus, *Fear and Hatred: Purifying Australia and California 1850-1901*, Hale & Iremonger, Sydney, 1979. Using parliamentary committee reports and contemporary newspapers, both reveal details about the Chinese communities of NSW and Victoria, such as clan

representation, the role of wealthy merchants, social organisations and the reality behind the many stereotypes held at the time. See for example, Price, op. cit., p.56, for a description of the 'commuting system' and p.218, for a discussion of visits to China.

⁹ A. Huck, *Chinese in Australia*, Longmans, Melbourne, 1968; C. Y. Choi, *Chinese Migration and Settlement in Australia*, Sydney University Press, Sydney, 1975. Choi gives a broader historical background and examines census data to reveal characteristics of the Chinese community. Choi, op. cit., p.84, also refers to the 'commuting system' and on p.87, to 'occasional visits'.

¹⁰ *Report of the Royal Commission on alleged Chinese Gambling & Immorality and charges of bribery against members of the police force,* Government Printer, Sydney, 1892.

¹¹ C. F. Yong, *The New Gold Mountain: the Chinese in Australia, 1901-1921*, Raphael Arts, Richmond, South Australia, 1977.

¹² Eric Rolls, *Sojourners: flowers and the wide sea,* vol.1, University of Queensland Press, St Lucia, 1992 & *Citizens: flowers and the wide sea,* vol.2, University of Queensland Press, St Lucia, 1996. Story telling is the aim and the lack of references and a critical framework makes this work less useful than it might otherwise have been; James Jupp (ed.), 'The Settlers: Chinese', in *The Australian People: An encyclopedia of the nation, its people and their origins,* Angus & Robertson, Sydney, 1988, pp.298-323.

¹³ Morag Jeanette Loh, *Dinky-di: the contributions of Chinese immigrants and Australians of Chinese descent to Australia's defence forces and war efforts 1899-1988*, Australian Government Publishing Service, Canberra, 1989. The impact of peoples' attitudes in both re-enforcing and also subverting the intent of formal restrictions is interesting, as is the insight this gives into the lives and families of Chinese Australians, see for example, Loh's interviews with Rosie Yuen and Yuen Hoy Poy in Loh, op. cit., pp.94-5 and p.101; Diana Giese, *Astronauts, Lost Souls & Dragons*, University of Queensland Press, St Lucia, 1997. See Giese, op. cit., pp.43-44, 137, 237 for examples. While interesting, a lack of critical framework limits the value of Giese's work.

¹⁴ Huang Tsen-ming, *The Legal Status of the Chinese Abroad: Overview of legal conditions in the US, British Empire, French and Dutch East Indies*, 2nd edn, China Cultural Service, Taipei, 1954; H. F. Macnair, *The Chinese Abroad*

Their Position and Protection. A Study in International Law and Relations, The Commercial Press, Shanghai, 1925; Chen Ta, *Chinese Migrations, with Special Reference to Labour Conditions*, Washington Government Printing Office, 1923; Persia Crawford Campbell, *Chinese Coolie Emigration to Countries Within the British Empire*, P.S. King & Sons, Westminster, 1923; Kay Saunders (ed.), *Indentured Labour in the British Empire 1834-1920*, Croom Helm, Canberra, 1984. These studies all deal with the mechanics of Chinese emigration, detailing the legal aspects, the distinction between indenture and the credit-ticket system and give us a glimpse of the harsh conditions under which many Chinese immigrated. Sources include many government studies that investigated Chinese immigration in attempts to ensure that compulsion was not part of it. The specifically Australian studies are, Jan Ryan, *Ancestors: Chinese in Colonial Australia,* Fremantle Arts Centre, Fremantle, 1995; Anne Atkinson, 'Chinese labour in Western Australia', *Time Remembered*, 6, 1984, pp.164-178 and Darnell, Maxine, The Chinese Labour Trade to New South Wales 1783-1853, PhD thesis, University of New England, 1997. The detail that Ryan has revealed based on material in Singapore might lead one to conclude that more can be found about this topic relating to Australia.

[15] Kathryn Cronin, *Colonial Casualties: Chinese in Early Victoria*, Melbourne University Press, Melbourne, 1982; Jean Gittins, *The Diggers from China: The story of the Chinese on the Goldfields,* Quartet Books, Melbourne, 1981. Gittins uses the diaries of China based European missionaries, but these do not add to the Chinese perspective.

[16] Cathie May, *Topsawyers: the Chinese in Cairns 1870 to 1920*, James Cook University, Townsville, 1984. May's use of sources, such as death and marriage registers, rate books, sugar mill records, school registers, oral accounts, the autobiographical writings of two Chinese merchants and even bank signature books, allows for the writing of a history of the Chinese of the Cairns district at a level quite different to any previous study.

[17] Diana Giese, *Beyond Chinatown,* National Library of Australia, Canberra, 1995.

[18] Ryan, op. cit. Ryan builds up a picture of a more diverse group of people with limited district links in comparison to Eastern States' Chinese communities. Ryan makes extensive use of

police and court records as well as the indenture records of the
Singapore based 'coolie' trade of the 19th century.

[19] Shirley Fitzgerald, *Red Tape, Gold Scissors,* State Library of
NSW Press, Sydney, 1997.

[20] Janis Wilton, Chinese Voices, Australian Lives, PhD thesis,
University of New England, 1996. Wilton, op. cit., p.34,
'visits to and contacts with China were an integral part of the
lives of Chinese-Australians living in the district'. Chapter 9,
'China', focuses on the relationship with China.

[21] I. Clunies Ross, *Australia and the Far East. History of Oriental
Trade Contacts and Diplomacy,* Australian Institute of
International Affairs, Angus and Robertson, 1935; Eric
Montgomery Andrews, *Australia and China: the ambiguous
relationship,* Melbourne University Press, Melbourne, 1985;
Sandra M. Tweedie, *Trading Partners: Australia and Asia
1790-1993,* University of New South Wales Press, Sydney,
1994; Wang Gungwu, *Community and Nation: China,
Southeast Asia, and Australia,* Asian Studies Association of
Australia in association with Allen & Unwin, Kensington,
1992. Tweedie and Andrews both make some reference to the
impact of the White Australia policy but neither have any
evidence beyond speculation. Margaret Tart, *The Life of
Quong Tart: or How a Foreigner Succeeded in a British
Community*, Sydney, 1911; Robert Travers, *Australian
Mandarin: the life and times of Quong Tart*, Kangaroo Press,
Kenthurst, 1981; Mo Yimei, *William J. Liu, O.B.E. -
Pathfinder, 1893-1983,* Australia-China Chamber of
Commerce and Industry of New South Wales, Canberra, 1991.
The Australian Dictionary of Biography has twelve references
to Chinese born people, including Quong Tart and two
children of European missionaries. *Australian Dictionary of
Biography*, vol.1 - vol.6, Melbourne University Press, Calton,
1966-1993. *[A search of the Australian Dictionary of
Biography in 2025 reveals 40 entries of people cited as having
"Chinese" heritage. The increase is partly due to more
careful assessment of heritage but additional biographies
have contributed most.]*

[22] Some studies of overseas Chinese businesses have been
undertaken, for example, Michael Godley, *The Mandarin-
capitalists from Nanyang: overseas Chinese enterprise in the
modernisation of China 1893-1911*, Cambridge University
Press, New York, 1981 and David Ch'ng, *The Overseas
Chinese Entrepreneurs in East Asia: background, business*

practices and international networks, Committee for Economic Development of Australia, Sydney, 1993. There would seem to be scope for similar studies in Australia and Wilton's research on the networks in the New England district indicates that much could be revealed.

23 Wellington K. K. Chan, 'The Organisational Structure of the Traditional Chinese Firm and its Modern Reform', *Business History Review*, vol.56, Summer, 1992, pp.218-235.

24 Some examples are: V. W. Purcell, *Chinese in Southeast Asia*, 2nd edn, Oxford University Press, 1966. *Nanyang* is the general Chinese term for South-East Asia and the Chinese emigrant communities there; Wang Gungwu, *China and the Chinese Overseas*, Times Academic Press, Singapore, 1991; and Anthony Reid (ed.), *Sojourners and Settlers: histories of Southeast Asia and the Chinese*, Asian Studies Association of Australia in association with Allen & Unwin, Sydney, 1996.

25 The first, that is, since the excellent and still valuable study by Chen Ta in the 1930s. Chen Ta, *Emigrant Communities in South China: A Study of Overseas Migration and its influence on standards of living and social change*, 2nd edn, Institute of Pacific Relations, New York, 1940.

26 Described in Lucie Cheng, 'Haiwai huaren yenjiu' (American Chinese Researches), *Qiaoshi xuebao*. no.1, June, 1989, p.232.

27 Y. F. Woon, 'An Emigrant Community in the Ssu-yi Area, Southeastern China, 1885-1949: A Study in Social Change', *Modern Asian Studies*, 18, 2, 1984, pp.273-306 and 'Social Change and Continuity in South China: Overseas Chinese and the Guan Lineage of Kaiping County, 1949-87', *China Quarterly*, 118, June, 1989, pp. 324-344; James L. Watson, *Emigration and the Chinese Lineage: the Mans in H.K. and London*, University of California Press, Berkeley, 1975.

28 A few examples of this research are: Feng Yuan 馮元, "Luelun jiefang qian guangdongsheng huaqiao huikuan" 論略解放前 廣東省 華僑匯款 (A brief discussion of Guangdong overseas Chinese remittances before liberation), *Qiaoshi xuebao* 僑史 學報 (Journal of Overseas Chinese History), 1, 1989, pp.31-40; Huang Chongyan 黃重言, "Yanjiu huaqiaoshi shang de jidian yijian" 研究華僑史上的幾點意見 (A few comments about researching overseas Chinese history), *Huaqiao lunwen shi* 華僑論文史 (Overseas Chinese History Thesis), No.1, April 1982, pp.24-28 and Huang Daoji 黃道記 & Liu

Chongmin 劉重民, "Taishanren shewai jiaowang yu chuyang suyuan" 台山人涉外交往與出洋溯源 (The origin of Taishan people's overseas migration and their links), *Qiaoshi xuebao* 僑史學報 (Journal of Overseas Chinese History), No.1, 1989, pp.7-8. The study by Elizabeth Sinn of Hong Kong's regional associations and the role of the Tung Wah Hospital raises interesting possibilities for comparisons with similar societies in Australia and their links with this Hospital. See Elizabeth Sinn, 'Xin Xi Guxiang: A Study of Regional Associations as a Bonding Mechanism in the Chinese Diaspora. The Hong Kong Experience', *Modern Asian Studies,* 31, 2, 1997, pp. 375-397 and *Power and Charity – The Early History of the Tung Wah Hospital, Hong Kong,* Oxford University Press, Hong Kong, 1989.

[29] That material relevant to Australia might be uncovered once research of Chinese sources is begun is suggested by a number of examples. The Kaiping Overseas Chinese Museum in 1985 collected over 400 items from families with overseas Chinese connections, in Kan Yanxin 闞延鑫, "Cong Kaiping huaqiao bowuguan wenwu cangpin, kan huaqiao dui zuguo de gongxian" 從開平華僑博物館文物藏品, 看華僑對祖國的貢獻 (From the collection of the Kaiping Museum to see the overseas Chinese contribution to the home country), *Qiaoshi xuebao* 僑史學報 (Journal of Overseas Chinese History), 1, 1987, p.44; also a reference to donations to China from Australian *huaqiao* in support of a port strike in 1925, found in the strike committee report and a reference to Quong Tart in the Mei family records in Hong Kong, see Huang Daoji 黃道記 & Liu Chongmin 劉重民, "Taishanren shewai jiaowang yu chuyang suyuan" 台山人涉外交往與出洋溯源 (The origin of Taishan people's overseas migration and their links), Qiaoshi xuebao 僑史學報 (Journal of Overseas Chinese History), No.1, 1989, pp.7-8. [For a limited move in this direction see D. Byrne, I. Ang, and P. Mar (eds), *Heritage and History in the China–Australia Migration Corridor*, Hong Kong University Press, 2023.)]

[30] H. D. Min-hsu Chan, 'A decade of achievement and future directions in research on the history of the Chinese in Australia', in Museum of Chinese Australian History, *Histories of the Chinese in Australasia and the South Pacific,*

Museum of Chinese Australian History, Melbourne, 1995, p.420.

[31] Both *huaqiao* and 'overseas Chinese' have a variety of meanings with historical and political implications and the best discussion of the general history of the term *huaqiao* and its changing meanings is that by Wang Gungwu, 'South China perspective's on overseas Chinese', *The Australian Journal of Chinese Affairs,* no.13, 1984, pp.69-84; see also, Fitzgerald, op. cit., pp.5-6, on defining 'Chineseness'.

[32] On northern NSW see, Wilton, op. cit., pp.4-5.

[33] Price, op. cit., p.220, n.12, gives district proportions for Sydney's *huaqiao* based on material drawn from files of the 1960s and 1970s. For a more detailed discussion of the evidence that proportions did change see, Appendix V.

[34] Barry York, *Admissions and Exclusions: 'Asiatics' and 'other coloured races' in Australia: 1901 to 1946,* Centre for Immigration & Multicultural Studies, Australian National University, 1995, Table 1.1, p.3.

[35] See Appendix IV for a general overview of the nature of these files; also Yarwood, op. cit., Chapter 3, pp.42-66; and Palfreeman, op. cit., pp.5-19 and Chapter 8, pp.81-101, for general discussion and administrative details.

[36] NAA: SP42/1; C1903/875, Mark Loong, Testimonial, 9 January 1903.

Chapter 1

[37] Chang Chung-li, *The Income of the Chinese Gentry*, University of Washington, Seattle, 1962, p.69.

[38] *Royal Commission*, op. cit., p.119, line, 4784 and p.145, line 5805.

[39] Choy op. cit., p.60, refers to secret society revolts in the 1842-55 period; p.61, the Taiping rebellion in 1854; pp.142-3, to inter-family feuds as late as 1898-9; and Appendix 1, pp.490-92, gives a table of disasters, including floods, famines and bandit attacks. Similar reasons are also recorded in the ancestor records about clan members who emigrated, see, Zheng Shanyu 鄭山玉, "Huaqiao yu hai shang sichou zhi lu - bufen qiaoxiang zupu zhong de haiwai yimin ziliao fenxi" 華僑與海上絲綢之路 - 部分僑鄉族譜中的海外移民資料分析 (Overseas Chinese and the Silk Road of the Sea - An analysis of overseas migration information of clan records in

part of the emmigrant communities), *Huaqiao huaren lishi yanjiu* 華僑華人歷史研究 (Overseas Chinese History Researches), No.1, 1991, pp.23-30 and in Zo Kil Young, 'Emigrant Communities in China, Sze-Yap', *Asian Profile*, vol.5, no.4, August, 1977, pp.313-23. In the 1930s, economic pressure was given as the principle cause of emigration in 70% of cases, Chen Ta, op. cit., pp.259-261, Table 26.

[40] Gunther Barth, *Bitter Strength*, Harvard University Press, Cambridge, Massachusetts, 1964. Chapter 3, describes this emigration as a model for that to California.

[41] Interview with Arthur Gar Lock Chang, Sydney, 7 March 1998. (Tape 1, B, 9.00). See Appendix II for an explanation of citations to interview transcripts and a brief outline of those interviewed.

[42] Map based on that in David Chuen-yan Lai, 'An analysis of data on home journeys by Chinese immigrants in Canada, 1892-1915', *The Professional Geographer*, 29.4, 1977, p.362.

[43] Choi, op. cit., pp.18-19; Price, op. cit., pp.76-89; and Fitzgerald, op. cit., pp.20-25. Just how early some Chinese were in Australia can be seen from the 'Deaths of Centenarians' tables which records, in 1911, the death at 105 of a Chinese born storekeeper of Gulgong who had been in Australia for 70 years, or since 1841; and in 1924 the death of a 127 year old Chinese gardener who had been in Australia 108 years, or since 1816. *Official Year Book of the Commonwealth of Australia*, no.6, 1901-1912, pp.217 & no.18, 1925, p.988.

[44] See Table 1, Appendix IV. Appendix IV also explains the sampling methods used to obtain all figures and statistics used in the thesis. On the scale of arrivals in the gold fields, Price, op. cit., p.88.

[45] Fitzgerald, op. cit., pp.67-9.

[46] This network of stores and societies is well illustrated in the *Royal Commission*, where there are numerous references scattered throughout the evidence to visits by the witnesses to such NSW towns as Hay, Hillston and Tingha and their Chinese 'camps'. Way Kee is reported to have had four stores in Bourke, Bega, Stanthorpe and Hillston, *Royal Commission*, op. cit., p.47, lines, 1704-8, and to send subscription books around the 'interior,' p.54, lines, 2056-83. See also Yong, op. cit., pp.39-41, for a discussion of the Chinese in the rural environment.

[47] The Hong Sing firm of Reservior St, Surry Hills sold to stores in Tenterfield, Emmaville and Tingha, see, NAA: SP1122/1; N57/2220, Chang Wai Sheu Sing. See also Wilton, op. cit., p.133, for details of northern NSW connections with Sydney. For details of imports see, NAA: A1026, Correspondence in connection with Immigration Restriction Act 1904-12, vol. 3, report, 'Check on importation of Chinese Goods', Collector of Customs to the Comptroller-General, 5 June 1908.

[48] *Royal Commission*, op. cit., p.115, lines, 4567-71, Sam Tin reported that as many as 50 stayed in his lodging house 'when they have been going away to China, or going into the country'. Victor Gow remembers he and his father in the 1920s staying above the Kwong War Chong store, 84 Dixon Street Sydney on buying trips from Wollongong. Interview with Victor Gow, 30 October 1997 (9).

[49] *Royal Commission*, op. cit., p.27, 'Callings and Occupations of the Chinese'. The 'Chinese Gambling Commission' was how the *Royal Commission*ers described themselves.

[50] *Royal Commission*, op. cit., p.28. See 'The Belmore Markets,' *Dalgety's Weekly*, 1 January 1902, p.85 for a description of Chinese in the markets; Yarwood, op. cit., p.117, thinks Chinese dominance was because such work was regarded as a, 'special preserve of the Chinese'; Price, op. cit., p.224, refers to greater efficiency compared to European gardeners; and 'Chinese in Sydney', *The Sydney Mail*, 25 February 1903, p.482, describes a Chinese Garden as, 'remarkable for the thorough manner in which it is worked. There is never a patch idle or weedy, …'

[51] Yarwood, op. cit., pp.117-119, on the banana trade, greengrocers and furniture trade; Yong, op. cit., p.52, on restrictions placed on Chinese in the banana trade and pp.70-77, on the anti-Chinese stores movement; Wilton, op. cit., pp.98-101, discusses the campaign against Chinese country stores. More recently Peter Gibson, *Made in Chinatown: Chinese Australian Furniture Factories, 1880-1930*, Sydney University Press, 2022 has written on cabinet making.

[52] Choi, op. cit., pp.28-9, pp.30-31 and p.52, refers to urbanisation and the growth of market gardening; Fitzgerald, op. cit., p.41, refers to migration to Sydney from rural areas and p.88, to the decline of the Rocks Chinatown and the rise of Haymarket as markets replace trade in importance; Wilton, op. cit., Diagram 1, p.77, illustrates the fall in Chinese numbers in one NSW region in the early 20th century.

53 *Royal Commission*, op. cit., p.93, line, 3698 and p.418, line, 15506.

54 See Appendix IV, Table 1 and 2.

55 NAA: ST84/1; Certificate Exempting From Dictation Test, 1904-1959.

56 See Appendix IV, Table 1.

57 *Royal Commission*, op. cit., p.57, line, 2220; Chen Ta, op. cit., p.131, referring to Southeast Asia states, 'The emigrant, at the time when he is leaving home, usually is an adolescent or in the early years of manhood.'

58 See Appendix IV, Table 5.

59 Choi, op. cit., p.13, and Price, op. cit., p.55 also discuss this aspect; Wilton, op. cit., pp.172-4, also mentions the tradition of male migration and a preference to leave wives in China.

60 Interview with Arthur Gar Lock Chang, Sydney, 7 March 1998 (Tape 2, B, 14.30); Baker, op. cit., p.35, refers to a 'white cockerel' as the traditional groom substitute in such proxy marriages.

61 Sinn, *Power and Charity,* op. cit., pp.55-6, contrasts the strength of the guild based structure of Hong Kong and Chinese cities generally with the importance of regional associations among the overseas Chinese.

62 *Royal Commission*, op. cit., p.28.

63 *Royal Commission*, op. cit., p.117, line, 4697.

64 According to Sinn, the purpose of such societies was also to express longing and to remind members of their obligations. Sinn, 'Xin Xi Guxiang', op. cit., p.375.

65 *Royal Commission*, op. cit., p.14, line, 402, 'The principal stores would be the treasury', and line, 404, 'the principal storekeepers would hold the money'. Norman Lee's father, Philip Lee Chun was the owner of the Kwong War Chong store and a founder of the Zhongshan society the Yum Duck Tong, interview with Norman Lee, Sydney, 25 September 1997 (11). Sinn, *Power and Charity*, op. cit., p.55, refers to the role of merchants in taking the place of the scholar elite in the circumstances of Hong Kong and p.60, discusses the characteristics of Chinese voluntary organisations.

66 *Royal Commission*, op. cit., p.47, lines, 1934-36.

67 *Royal Commission*, op. cit., p.52, line, 1946.

68 See, Leo J. Moser, *The Chinese Mosaic. The Peoples and Provinces of China*, Westview, London, 1985, pp.203-5 & 215, for a general discussion of Pearl River Delta dialects; David Faure & Helen Siu, *Down to Earth. The Territorial*

Bond in South China, Stanford University Press, Stanford, California, 1995, Introduction, p.11, discusses the complexity of South China's dialects; J. M. Rhoads, *China's Republican Revolution – The Case of Kwangtung, 1895-1913,* Harvard University Press, Cambridge, Massachusetts, 1975, pp.12-14, discusses the tensions created by dialect differences; Choy op. cit., pp.90-1, discusses the importance of dialect in unifying groups and Somers Heidhues, op. cit., pp.49-51, refers to the, 'natural division of overseas Chinese along speech groups'.

[69] Moser, op. cit., p.208, discusses the arrival of the Hakka in South China, p.216, their dialect enclaves and p.199, the dialect enclave of Long Dou; Choy op. cit., p.95, mentions six Zhongshan dialects and p.114, Longhua (the Longdu dialect).

[70] Interview with Donald Young, Sydney, 11 October 1997 (6) & Arthur Gar Lock Chang, 7 March 1998 (Tape 1, B, 0.84).

[71] *Royal Commission*, op. cit., p.146, lines, 5871-2.

[72] *Royal Commission*, op. cit., p.69, line, 2697 and p.117, line, 4665.

[73] *Royal Commission*, op. cit., p.115. Yong, op. cit., p.46, discusses this feature of the stores.

[74] Interview with Arthur Gar Lock Chang, Sydney, 7 March 1998 (Tape 2, B, 0.00).

[75] Interview with Arthur Gar Lock Chang, Sydney, 7 March 1998 (Tape 2, B, 0.75) & Victor Gow, 30 October 1997 (9).

[76] Yong, op. cit., p.46, considers that some were established with Hong Kong capital.

[77] NAA: SP42/1; C29/48, Ping Fun, Certificate of Registration of a firm with the Registrar-General, Sun Sam Choy – General Merchants, no.3, 694, 5 June 1906.

[78] Gao Minchuan 高民川, "Zhongshanshi huaqiao dashiji" 中山市華僑大事記 (Record of major events of Zhongshan City overseas Chinese), *Zhongshan wenshi* 中山文史 (Zhongshan Cultural History), Vol.20, 1990, p.11; and interview with Norman Lee, 25 September 1997 (2).

[79] NAA: SP42/1; N59/3386 Kwong War Chong & Co., 'Particulars form', 30 October 1951.

[80] For the attitude of Sydney *huaqiao* towards Europeans and their culture see, Yu Lan Poon, 'The two-way mirror: contemporary issues as seen through the eyes of the Chinese language press, 1901-1911', Chapter 3, pp.50-65, in Shirley Fitzgerald & Garry Wotherspoon, (ed.), *Minorities: cultural diversity in Sydney,* State Library of New South Wales Press

in association with the Sydney History Group, Sydney, 1995. See, NAA: SP1655/7; N53/24/3574, Choy On, letter, Deputy Crown Solicitor to Crown Solicitor, 24 November 1937, for references in a court case to poor English among Sydney Chinese in the 1930s as 'well known' and no proof of recent illegal entry. For a larrikin attack near Bondi and a description of English classes see, Margaret Egerton, 'My Chinese', op. cit., Sept, p.126 & Nov, p.193. For a general discussion of racism at the end of the nineteenth century, see Price, op. cit., pp.49-51.

[81] Sinn, *Power & Charity*, op. cit., p.14, on the wide role played in social organisation of the 'family, clan, and village'. Fitzgerald, op. cit., p.67, makes the point that such co-operation did not necessarily mean that no one found themselves without support.

[82] See, 'Chinese Merchants reply', *Sydney Morning Herald*, 22 August 1904, p.12, for a refutation of these claims against stores made by the Anti-Chinese and Asiatic League, including a table of typical expenses for a Chinese and European store in which the inclusion of boarding costs makes the Chinese store more expensive to operate.

[83] NAA: SP11/16; Aliens Registration 1916-21, Item no. 2, No.2 Police Station, Regents St, Sydney to Department of Defence, 8 December 1916. Also, Fitzgerald, op. cit., p.84, for a discussion of Ah Toy's workshop. Not that Chinese were the only workers to accept board, Thomas Smith, *Royal Commission*, op. cit., p.420, lines, 15635-15639, gave evidence of paying his two European workers 18s plus board while his Chinese worker received 26s without board.

[84] T. A. Coghlan, *NSW Statistical Register for 1899 and Previous Years,* Government Printer, Sydney, 1900, p.994, Part XIV, Industrial Wages, Table no. 7, and p.1004, Table no. 11. Though the rate for cooks in 1912 was reported as 30s per week and that for 'Chinese Cooks' as 40s! *NSW Statistical Register, 1919-20*, no.51, 'Average Rate of Wages in Misc. Industries, 1912,' p.486.

[85] NAA: SP726/1; Particulars of Applications for CEDTs, vol.1-vol.6. Sydney figures cannot be isolated, as people throughout NSW needed to pass through Sydney Port. The use of Brisbane and Melbourne by *huaqiao* living in NSW makes even trying to isolate NSW problematic.

[86] Fitzgerald, op. cit., p.26, and a discussion of ticket arrangements in the 1880s.

[87] This method has been described by many researchers, see Huck, op. cit., pp.3-4; Choi, op. cit., p.14; Price, op. cit., p.58; Yong, op. cit., p.1, quotes a 1857 Victorian parliamentary committee report that estimated two-thirds of the Chinese migrants of the time had arrived by this method.

[88] Fitzgerald, op. cit., p.27.

[89] *Royal Commission*, op. cit., p.27.

[90] *Royal Commission*, op. cit., p.160, lines, 6420-35. The Poll Tax was introduced under the 'Chinese Restriction and Regulation Act of 1888'. Price *op cit.* p.271, summaries this Act's impact and those of the other colonies at this time.

[91] Chen Ta, op. cit., p.131, reports that an emigrant would, 'remain single, especially if they have failed to improve their economic status' and p.135, that higher betrothal payments were expected of emigrant sons.

[92] *Royal Commission*, op. cit., p.419, lines, 15566-70. This was in the late nineteenth century, by the 1930s the gap had widened even more when according to, Chen Hen-Seng, *Landlord and Peasant in China – A Study of the Agrarian crisis in South China*, 2nd edn, Hyperion Press, Westport, Connecticut, 1973, p.103, it took a labourer 5 days in the 1930s to earn the price of a *mu* of land [rice field measure] in Canada compared to 8 years in Guangdong Province.

[93] *Royal Commission*, op. cit., p.55, line, 2126; Fitzgerald, op. cit., p. 47, refers to an early mishap which may have encouraged the use of a safer system.

[94] Interview with Arthur Gar Lock Chang, 7 March 1998 (Tape 1, B, 3.33); Yong, op. cit., pp.46-7, quotes an example from the *Chinese Australian Herald* of these services provided by the store On Yik & Lee.

[95] Interview with Norman Lee, Sydney, 25 September 1997 (1 & 10) and NAA: SP42/1; N59/3386, Kwong War Chong & Co., 'Particulars form', 30 October 1951.

[96] The Kwong War Chong was used, for example, by Victor Gow and his father. Interview with Victor Gow, Sydney, 30 October 1997 (9). Wing On & Co. was used by Lee Man Dick, Cliff Lee's father. Interview with Cliff Lee, Sydney, 28 September 1997 (1 & 6).

[97] NAA: C4203/1; Department of Custom & Excise, NSW, Boarding Branch Records of Files & Orders, 1914-31, vol.1, p.35, memo, Comptroller-General, Department of Trade & Customs to Collector of Customs, 3 March 1916.

[98] Interview with Norman Lee, Sydney, 25 September 1997 (2). When the Bank of China began to take over all remittances it issued a standard letter form to accompany remittances that may well have been modelled on that created by the stores' scribes. Such a letter had 5 points: best wishes, write more often, let me know when received, have received your letter and tell how to spend the money in another letter. Mar Letters, no.264, Bank of China notice, 5 June 1944.

[99] Interview with Norman Lee, Sydney, 25 September 1997 (2,3 &4). Miao Wenyue 繆文雨 & Gao Huanzhang 高煥章, "Shiqi yinye de huiyi" 石岐銀業的回憶 (Recollections of the Shiqi silver industry), *Zhongshan wenshi* 中山文史 (Zhongshan Cultural History), Vol.1-3, [1962-1965], 1989, pp.88-95, discusses the commissions earned between Shiqi and Hong Kong. Compare the similar descriptions of remittance services in Hawaii, Char, op. cit., p127; and Chen Ta, op. cit., p.79, the *nanyang*,. The Tiy Loy & Co. of the Gao Yao people in Sussex St. Sydney still has such a letter rack, though now used only for correspondence. [While little is said about Australia, an excellent history of the remittance system of the Chinese diaspora can be found in Gregor Benton & Hong Liu, *Dear China Emigrant Letters and Remittances, 1820–1980*, University of California Press, 2018.]

[100] Interview with Norman Lee, Sydney, 25 September 1997 (5).

[101] *Royal Commission*, op. cit., p.395, lines, 14333-14337.

[102] Interview with Cliff Lee, 28 September 1997 (1).

[103] Arthur Gar Lock Chang, 7 March 1998 (Tape 1, A, 9.30).

[104] Interview with Billy Gay, 19 March 1998 (Tape 1, B, 200).

[105] Interview with Victor Gow, 30 October 1997 (5) and Arthur Gar Lock Chang, 7 March 1998 (Tape 1, A, 9.30).

[106] NAA: SP42/1; C1903/5280, Tommy Way, letter from Manager, Onyik Lee & Co. to Collector of Customs, NSW, 25 May 1902. Max Weber, *The Religion of China*, The Macmillan Co., New York, 1964, p.123, considers children's education in traditional China to consist largely to encourage, 'piety and awe towards parents'.

[107] Numerous references found in NAA: SP42/1. As the century progresses mention of visits to parents are replaced by those to wife and family but seemingly only after the parents had died.

[108] Also, Choi, op. cit., pp.48-49, discusses marriages in Australia and China.

[109] *Official Year Book of the Commonwealth of Australia*, Commonwealth Bureau of Census and Statistics, Melbourne, 1925, Table 10, no.18, p.956.

[110] Joe Wah Gow even managed to marry an Australian born Chinese girl that he met in China, interview with Victor Gow, 30 October 1997 (3).

[111] Choi, op. cit., p.49, 'The traditional commuting system, plus the restrictive legislation, virtually forced single Chinese men wishing to marry Chinese women to return to their places of origin to marry.'

[112] See, Yarwood, op. cit., pp.79-81 for a discussion of these amendments and their reasons.

[113] *Royal Commission*, op. cit., p.58, lines, 2239-40 and p.57, line 2213.

[114] *Royal Commission*, op. cit., p.396, line, 14400.

[115] Wilton, op cit. pp.174-7, gives examples of strategies used to extend short-term visits for wives.

[116] NAA: SP1122/1; N57/2220, Chang Wau Sheu Sing.

[117] *Royal Commission*, op. cit., p.397, lines, 14424-29.

[118] Interview with Billy Gay, 19 March 1998 (Tape 1, A, 70 & 210).

[119] Interview with Norman Lee, 25 September 1997 (1).

[120] Interview with Norman Lee, 25 September 1997 (7).

[121] The census was recording formal marriages only. On the question of attitudes to marriage and intermarriage see, Price, op. cit., pp.108-9 & 249; and Wilton, op. cit., p.164. For a case of a Chinese father's opposition to his daughter marrying a 'white,' that was well publicised in 1946, see, NAA: SP1655; N54/24/3362, Gwenda Yee.

[122] Concubinage was legally ended only after 1930, Choi, op. cit., p.37.

[123] *Royal Commission*, op. cit., p.481, Appendix C.

[124] *Royal Commission*, op. cit., p.74, lines, 2933-36.

[125] NAA: SP1122/1; 53/24/3495, Chan Young Sow, memo 5 June 1963.

[126] NAA: SP1122/1; N56/818, Yee Bun War (William Bun), application, 17 May 1956.

[127] Interview with Cliff Lee, 28 September 1997 (8) & Norman Lee 25 September 1997 (7). Fitzgerald, op. cit., p.164, discusses the 'old men' in the 1950s and 60s, and quotes King Fong, 'Some of the old men sold peanuts at Randwick races, in baskets once used for vegies'.

[128] *Royal Commission*, op. cit., p.395, lines, 14347-57; Yong, op. cit., Chapter 10, pp. 171-72, discusses the effect of the lack of family life; and Wilton, op. cit., pp.142-6, discusses opium and gambling in the 'Bachelor Society' of northern NSW.

[129] Paul C. P. Siu, 'The Sojourner', *The American Journal of Sociology*, LVII, July, 1952, p.42, reports on the consequences for the sojourner of 'personal disorganisation'.

Chapter 2

[130] NAA: SP1122/1; N53/24/2293, Foo Chong, reference 28 June 1924.

[131] Norman Lee confirms this general pattern, interview with Norman Lee, 25 September 1997 (7). Price, op. cit., p.218, also considers 1-2 years an average stay. That such a pattern was typical of *huaqiao* elsewhere is confirmed by a description of the sojourning of the *huaqiao* of Hawaii, who also came largely from Zhongshan district. 'Some [Chinese farmers], after a stay in their native land, returned to Hawaii, earned more money and again went home. Others took trips to China every two to three years, going back five or six times before their final return to their homeland.' 'They wanted to earn as much money as they could as quickly as possible and return to their native land, either to invest or to spend it...' Char, op. cit., p.95.

[132] Interview with Billy Gay, 19 March 1998 (Tape 2, A 115).

[133] NAA: SP1122/1; N53/24/2504, Lee Man Dick (Man Duck) and interview with Cliff Lee, 28 September 1997 (1).

[134] Photo taken by author with permission of Cliff Lee, Jin Huan village, Zhongshan, January 1998.

[135] Yarwood says this is because the Immigration Restriction Act had always been designed to be based on 'administrative techniques' and this required the administrators to look to the debates rather than the wording of the Act itself. In addition, the ALP used its influence to ensure that administration of the Act was tight. See, Yarwood, op. cit., pp.22-3, and pp.68-70, where he discusses the early interpretation of the Act. [For a complete history of the administration of the Dictation Test see, Michael Williams, *Australia's Dictation Test: The Test it was a Crime to Fail*, Brill, 2021.]

[136] NAA: SP42/1; C1902/4116, William Wong Gip, report by J. T.

T. Donohoe, 13 June 1902.

[137] NAA: SP42/1; C1903/5280, Tommy Way, letter, manager Onyik Lee & Co. to Collector of Customs, 25 May 1902. Tommy Way was applying to re-enter Australia without a Certificate of Domicile and the manager of Onyik Lee & Co. wrote a letter explaining why he, and others, had not applied on departure.

[138] NAA: A1; 1903/3081, Instructions re: Certificate of Domiciles, minute, 26 November 1902.

[139] See, 'Chinese delegation to the Prime Minister', *Daily Telegraph*, 30 December 1902, for an example of this. Yarwood, op. cit., pp.69-70, considers the March 1903 suspension of the wives exemption to have allowed a more relaxed attitude to the domiciles.

[140] NAA: SP42/1; C1903/903, War Sing, letter, Braye & Cohen to Collector of Customs, 6 February 1903.

[141] NAA: SP42/1; C1903/5280, Tommy Way, letter, manager Onyik Lee & Co. to Collector of Customs, 25 May 1902.

[142] NAA: SP42/1; C31/1130, Ah Way, letter, Joe Que to Collector of Customs, 6 November 1910.

[143] NAA: A1026; Correspondence re Immigration Act 1904-12, vol. 2, p.34, letter Acting Collector of Customs to Master of Lunacy, Supreme Court, 22 January 1907.

[144] NAA: A1026; Correspondence re Immigration Act 1904-12, vol. 3, p.341, report, 'Chinese Goods - Check on Importations', the Acting Collector of Customs to the Comptroller-General, 5 June 1908. For 1962, see NAA: A6980/T1; S250386, 'Non European Policy Review 1962'.

[145] Official Year Book of the Commonwealth of Australia, no.18, 1925, Section 14, 'Chinese in Australia', pp.951-956. See Appendix 1, Table 1 for figures from the nineteenth century to 1947.

[146] Palfreeman, op. cit., p.6, refers to the removal of 'statutory sanctions' in 1905 and the continuance of domicile returns without them.

[147] NAA: SP42/1; C1903/1577, Kee Sun, report, 28 February 1903.

[148] NAA: SP42/1; C1916/4346, She Jin, memo, 22 July 1914 and letter, Atlee Hunt Secretary, Department of External Affairs, to Collector of Customs, 1916.

149 NAA: SP1122/1; C33/7368, Harry Chun Fook, report, Investigating Officer to Boarding Inspector, 19 September 1933.

150 NAA: SP1122/1; C33/7368, Harry Chun Fook, letter, Secretary to Collector of Customs, 4 September 1933.

151 NAA: A1026; Correspondence re Immigration Act 1904-12, vol.1, p.67, letter, Collector of Customs to Rev T.O. Todd, 7 February 1906.

152 NAA: SP42/1; C11/1113, Yet Hing & C1913/7010, Yook Fong.

153 NAA: SP42/1; C19/7011, William Ah Ping, memo, 8 September 1919.

154 NAA: SP42/1; C20/1147, Norman Charles Aubrey Mar Young.

155 'The Influx of Chinese Restriction Act of 1881'. See, NAA: SP115/10; Certificates of Residence 1862-1886, Ung Hoe 1885 (1002), for a certificate issued under this Act.

156 NAA: SP42/1; C29/40, Jow Kue, Ah Yaut, letter, Ben Hing to the Collector of Customs, 12 May 1907. It was a common practice for Chinese firms to sign a letter with the company name regardless of the name of the actual manager writing the letter.

157 NAA: SP42/1; C29/40, Jow Kue, Ah Yaut.

158 NAA: SP42/1; C29/40 Jow Kue, Ah Yaut.

159 NAA: C4203/1; Boarding Branch Records, 1914-1931, vol.2, p.353, Circular, Secretary to Collector of Customs, 25 February 1924.

160 NAA: SP1122/1; N52/24/314, Ah Moy (Mhoy) and SP42/1; C47/2468, Yum Leong.

161 NAA: SP42/1; C13/1663, statement and papers in case of five people rejected for entry, record of interview of Ah Shing, 31 March 1913.

162 NAA: SP1122/1; N53/24/2343, Ah Tom, memo re number of blank CEDTs stolen by Departmental Officer, 3 August 1953; also Yarwood, op. cit., p.62, refers to evidence of Customs officials involvement in illegal entry.

163 NAA: SP42/1; C1903/1980, Jee Kwong & C11/703, Lois Poy. According to Yarwood, op. cit., p.54, NSW was a 'haven' for Chinese deserters, and pp.56-57, gives figures for 1914 that 77 of 81 deserters were in NSW due to ships staying longer in Sydney and the greater number of Chinese there making hiding easier.

[164] NAA: SP42/1; C11/392, Crew Muster Report, memo, Boarding Inspector to Collector of Customs, Brisbane, 21 January 1911.

[165] Between 1926 and 1929, 400 people were deported as stowaways, Fitzgerald, op. cit., p.32.

[166] NAA: A1026; Correspondence re Immigration Act 1904-12, vol. 1, p.12, letter, the Collector of Customs to Manager, Burns Philp & Co., 10 January 1906 & vol. 3, p.328, memo, Detective Inspector to Boarding Inspector, 23 March 1908.

[167] NAA: A1026; Correspondence re Immigration Act 1904-12, vol. 3, p.347, report, 'Chinese Goods - Check on Importations', Revenue Detective Inspector to the Acting Collector of Customs, 5 June 1908; Yarwood, op. cit., pp.56-62, also details efforts to catch stowaways.

[168] NAA: A1026; Correspondence re Immigration Act 1904-12, vol. 3, p.347, report, 'Chinese Goods - Check on Importations', Revenue Detective Inspector to the Acting Collector of Customs, 15 April 1908.

[169] NAA: C3939/2; N1962/75101, 'Summary and statistics of activities associated with illegals or prohibited Chinese immigrants in NSW'.

[170] NAA: SP740/1; NN George Gay & Lee Bung Yee, bonds, 15 March 1923.

[171] NAA: SP1122/1; C47/2352, Leong Hoi Cheng, letter, George Mook to the Collector of Customs, Newcastle, 14 December 1944.

[172] NAA: C4203/1; Boarding Branch Records, 1914-1931, vol.2, p.460, circular, Assistant Secretary to Collector of Customs, 4 March 1927.

[173] NAA: SP42/1; C33/6955, Lum Bow, Lee Fook.

[174] NAA: SP42/1; C33/7556, Kwok Yen Fong, memo, Detective Inspector to Boarding Inspector, 15 August 1933.

[175] NAA: SP1148/2; Passenger lists, Outgoing 1929 & 1939.

[176] NAA: SP42/1; C33/7574, Ah Lee, letter, Eastern and Australian Steamship Co. to the Collector of Customs, 30 June 1921.

[177] Billy Gay estimated that £2 per week in the 1930s was a 'good wage' for a market gardener. Interview with Billy Gay, 19 March 1998 (Tape 2, A, 115).

[178] NAA: SP1148/2; Passenger lists, Outward 1902, 1929 & 1939.

[179] Interview with Arthur Gar Lock Chang, Sydney, 7 March

1998 (Tape 2, B, 150).

[180] Noel Butlin Archives Centre (ANU); Deposit E217/628, Shipowners Chamber, Newspaper cuttings, p.142, Age clipping, 25 February 1931.

[181] Interview with Arthur Gar Lock Chang, Sydney, 7 March 1998 (Tape 2, B, 9.00).

[182] Interview with Billy Gay, Sydney, 19 March 1998 (Tape 1, B, 200) & Arthur Gar Lock Chang, Sydney, 7 March 1998 (Tape 2, B, 9.00).

[183] *Royal Commission*, op. cit., p.99, lines, 3982-83.

[184] NAA: SP42/1; C11/1161, Ah Pong.

[185] NAA: SP115/1; *Taiping* 2/6/29 & *Arafura* 30/5/29; NAA: SP115/1; *Taiping*, 4/8/29.

[186] NAA: SP42/1; C13/639, Tarm Hew, note of interview, 7 February 1913.

[187] Interview with Cliff Lee, 28 September 1997 (3).

[188] Interview with Arthur Chang, 7 March 1998 (Tape 2, A, 3.22) & Cliff Lee, 28 September 1997 (7)

[189] Photo taken by author with permission of Cliff Lee, Jin Huan village, Zhongshan, January 1998.

[190] Interview with Arthur Gar Lock Chang, 7 March 1998 (Tape 1, A, 4.00)

[191] NAA: SP42/1; C31/980, Wong Yong, file note, 2 January 1930.

[192] Chen Hen-Seng, op. cit., p.3, 18 & 62, for the impact on land prices of overseas remittances and pp.87-96, on peasant loss of land due to debt. Also, Chen Ta, op. cit., p.18, 62, 67 & pp.84-5.

[193] Chen Hen-Seng, op. cit., pp.22, 47-8, on the higher incidence of sub-renting in Chungshan (Zhongshan) and other districts; Faure, op. cit., p.205, discusses the complexities of the landlord/tenant relationships.

[194] Chen Hen-Seng, op. cit., p.48, on speculation in rice.

[195] Interview with Arthur Gar Lock Chang, 28 October 1997 (Tape 1, A, 12.00) & Cliff Lee, Zhongshan, 7 January 1998; Chen Hen-Seng, op. cit., p.54, reports that cash rents were more common in Zhongshan than most other districts.

[196] Chen Ta, op. cit., p.121, gives examples of families and the role of the wife 'acting head of the family' while the husband was overseas; Chen Hen-Seng, op. cit., pp.46-8, on leasing

details, such as deposits and sub-tenants.

[197] Chen Ta, op. cit., pp.175-182, analyses the prevalence of these diseases in the villages of south China.

[198] Chen Ta, op. cit., pp.187-192 describes the relationship of these habits with 'emigrant communities'; Zheng Dehua 鄭德華, "Shijiu shiji mo Taishan qiaoxiang de xingcheng ji qi pouxi" 十九世紀末台山僑鄉的形成及其剖析 (A analysis of the formation of overseas emigrant communities in Taishan in the late 19th century), *Qiaoshi xuebao* 僑史學報 (Journal of Overseas Chinese History), No.3, 1986, p.36.

[199] Chen Ta, op. cit., Table 5, pp.82-85, shows among a survey of emigrant families that 75% to 85% of family income was from remittances. Also Lin Jinzhi 林金枝, "Cong zupu ziliao kan min yue renmin yiju haiwai de huodong ji qi dui jiaxiang de gongxian" 從族譜資料看閩粵人民移居海外的活動及其對家鄉的貢獻 (A look at clan records to see the overseas activities of Fujian and Guangdong people and their contribution to their hometowns), *Huaqiao huaren lishi yanjiu* 華僑華人歷史研究 (Overseas Chinese History Researches), 1, 1991, pp.16-23. It should be remembered that the *huaqiao* and emigration were not the concern of the majority of the population of Guangdong, Chen Hen-Seng, op. cit., pp.110-111, has calculated that in the 1920s and 30s more peasants left their villages to join the 19th Route Army than emigrated.

[200] Interview with Arthur Gar Lock Chang, Sydney, 7 March 1998 (Tape 1, A, 14.00).

[201] The Kwoks established the now multinational Wing On Co.

[202] Photo courtesy of Victor Gow. Taken in the 1960s, Long Tou Wan village, Zhongshan.

[203] Chen Ta, op. cit., pp.46-49, on donations, and pp.192-4, refers to the impact of the *huaqiao* in terms of ideas and innovations, particularly in such areas as education and the adoption of sports such as soccer.

[204] Victor Gow, 30 October 1997 (4). Chen Ta, op. cit., pp.149-60, on the importance and role of education & pp.162-166, on the financial arrangements of *huaqiao* organised schools; Choy, op. cit., pp.257-60, on the history of one *huaqiao* clan's support for schools from the mid-18th century and the tendency of their educated members to go into business rather than complete their degrees in the 19th century; and Yu Renqiu, 'Chinese American Contributions to the Educational

Development of Toisan 1910-1940', *Amerasia Journal* 10/1, 1983, pp.47-72, for an overview of Taishan *huaqiao's* contribution to their districts education.

[205] Victor Gow, 30 October 1997 (4). One of Joe Wah Gow's daughters became a doctor and she and her doctor husband currently [1998] run a weekend clinic in the village. They plan to convert the house built by Joe Wah Gow into a new clinic for the village.

[206] Interview with Arthur Gar Lock Chang, 7 March 1998 (Tape 1, B, 9.00).

[207] Interview with Norman Lee, 25 September 1997 (13).

[208] Interview with Cliff Lee, 28 September 1997 (7). Gao Minchuan 高民川, "Zhongshanshi huaqiao dashiji" 中山市華僑大事記 (Record of major events of Zhongshan City overseas Chinese), *Zhongshan wenshi* 中山文史 (Zhongshan Cultural History), Vol.20, 1990, p.19, mentions support from Philip Kwok, the Wing On founder, to his home village in 1921.

[209] Miao Wenyue 繆文雨 & Gao Huanzhang 高煥章, "Shiqi yinye de huiyi" 石岐銀業的回憶 (Recollections of the Shiqi silver industry), *Zhongshan wenshi* 中山文史 (Zhongshan Cultural History), Vol.1-3, [1962-1965], 1989, p.93 and ,高民川 Gao Minchuan, op. cit., p.21.

[210] NAA: SP42/1; C31/535, Lee Yip Fay, letter, Lee Yip Fay to Collector of Customs, 15 May 1928; Chen Ta, op. cit., p.20, quotes a report on the increase in *nanyang huaqiao* investment in their home districts after 1911 and the general failure of these investments due to 'disturbances', and pp.75-76, on the later preference for keeping capital elsewhere due to China's instability.

[211] NAA: SP42/1; C31/135, Lee Yip Fay, letter, Lee Yip Fay to Collector of Customs, 15 May 1928.

[212] See Rhoads, op. cit., p.40, for the 1895 republican uprising in Zhongshan involving Sun Yat-sen, pp.146-7, for the 1905-10 dispute with Macao, p.176, for the 1910 riot and destruction of a tax office in Shekki and pp.257-61, for the 1912-13 land equalisation reform in Guangdong and its suppression; Chen Ta, op. cit., p.162, on the military conflict in 1923 between Guangdong and Fujian provinces and p.224, on bandits and communist uprisings generally; Choi, op. cit., p.8, for the 'Farmer's Movement' in the 1920s; Helen Siu, 'Subverting Lineage Power, op. cit., p.195, for attacks on Shekki by bandit

'fleets' in 1915 and 1922; Chen Hen-Seng, op. cit., pp.xiii-ix, on military based landlords and the rise in taxes, rents and land prices in the 1920-30s.

[213] 'Banditti' are mentioned in Heängshan (Zhongshan) in 1832, *Chinese Repository*, vol. 1, no.1, May, 1832, p.80.

[214] Especially after the 'peoples' armies' that had helped win the republican cause in Guangdong province were disbanded during 1912-13, Rhoads, op. cit., pp.239-40; Helen F. Sui, *Agents and Victims in South China – Accomplices in Rural Revolution*, Yale University Press, New Haven & London, 1989, pp.88-115, discusses how the Republicans by-passed the traditional town elites, giving rise to local strongmen; see also Wilton, op. cit., p.216, for some personal accounts of bandit attacks.

[215] Helen Siu, 'Subverting Lineage Power', op. cit., pp.188-9 & p.195.

[216] Chen, op. cit., pp. 81, 96 & 104-5.

[217] Interview with Arthur Gar Lock Chang, 7 March 1998 (Tape 1, B, 14.00).

[218] Helen Siu, 'Subverting Lineage Power', in Faure & Siu, op. cit., p.195.

[219] See Helen Siu, 'Subverting Lineage Power', op. cit., p.195, on the breaking of lineage power in Zhongshan as local bosses linked to warlords directly levied taxes and Helen Sui, *Agents and Victims*, op. cit., pp.88-96, on the reign of the local bosses, tax collection and black & red tickets.

[220] Interview with Arthur Gar Lock Chang, 7 March 1998 (Tape 1, B, 15.00). See also, Helen Siu, 'Subverting Lineage Power', in Faure & Siu, op. cit., pp.191-2, on the role of the local bosses between the Japanese and Nationalists.

[221] Interview with Arthur Gar Lock Chang, 7 March 1998 (Tape 1, B, 18.00)

[222] Chen Ta, op. cit., pp.197-201, on the *huaqiao* contribution to village defence. Sinn, *Power and Charity*, p.27, refers to Chinese communities providing their own police as customary.

[223] Victor Gow, 30 October 1997 (13).

[224] Interview with Arthur Gar Lock Chang, 28 October 1997 (12). Chen Hen-Seng, op. cit., p.81, refers to special taxes for building of watch-towers.

[225] Interview with Cliff Lee, 28 September 1997 (2).

[226] Interview with Cliff Lee, Jan 1998, Zhongshan City.

227 NAA: SP1122/1; N67/4101, Kwok Pearl (Mrs).

228 Photo taken by author in Jin Huan Village, Zhongshan, January 1998.

229 林顺忠 Lin Shunzhong & 孙德才 Sun Decai, 沙边村的碉楼 'Shabiancun de Diaolou' (Towers of Shabian Village), 中山日报Zhongshan Ribao (Zhongshan newspaper), 20 December 1997. Also personal observation during field trip in Zhongshan district, January, 1998.

230 Interview with Arthur Gar Lock Chang, 7 March 1998 (Tape 1, A, 14.00).

231 See Chen Ta, op. cit., pp.175-180, on the presence of plague, smallpox, cholera and other diseases in the villages of south China in the 1930s.

232 ibid., p.202, 'Returned emigrants from Australia and America sometimes were able to found new communities.'

233 Sinn, op. cit., pp.100 & 111-2, and p.163, on the role of educated overseas merchants and p.169, on the role of an Australian born *huaqiao* specifically.

234 NAA: SP1122/1; N53/24/2284, Choy See Pan Kee (Mrs Thomas Pan Kee) & N53/24/2285-90, files of the Pan Kee children, Lawrence, Rose, Agnes, Minnie and Mary.

235 NAA: SP1122/1; N67/4101, Kwok Pearl (Mrs) (Pearl Lock Lee).

236 Interview with Cliff Lee, 28 September 1997 (5). As Baker put it, 'it was essential for the rich to keep away from the village', Baker, op. cit., p.174.

237 Victor Gow, 30 October 1997 (6).

238 NAA: SP42/2, C1933/4302, Edna Lock Lee.

Chapter 3

239 Mar letter: no. 284. Letter, Wing On manager, Sydney to Chiang Kai-Shek, 6 June 1939. Translation by Chen Mei-Su.

240 NAA: SP42/1; C47/2352, Leong Hoi Cheng, memo, H. E. Smith, 24 January 1945.

241 NAA: SP115/1; Arafura, 30 May 1929, Passenger lists.

242 Choi, op. cit., pp.45-6, analyses census data to estimate the retirement pattern of the over 60s. Stephen Fitzgerald, *China and the Overseas Chinese; a study of Peking's changing policy, 1949-1970,* Cambridge University Press, 1972, p.69, estimates that 500,000 *huaqiao* returned to China between 1949 and 1966, including many retirees.

[243] NAA: SP1148/2; Passenger lists, Outward 1929 & Table 10, Appendix IV.

[244] Interviews with Billy Gay, 19 March 1998 (Tape 1, B, 300); King Fong, 1 April 98 (interview notes); Cliff Lee, 28 September 1997 (8); Fitzgerald, op. cit., p.164.

[245] Interview with King Fong, 1 April 1998 (interview notes) and Billy Gay, 19 March 1998 (Tape 1, B, 300). Rent receipt books of the Say Tin Co., 1970-1983, in the possession of Mr. King Fong.

[246] Freedman, op. cit., pp.139-140, on the role of bones in ancestor worship. Sinn, *Power & Charity*, op. cit., p.18, considers that concern for the dead was 'paramount' with the overseas Chinese.

[247] The *Chinese Australian Herald* (廣益華報), 3 June 1903, p.3.

[248] *Royal Commission*, op. cit., p.55, line, 2113.

[249] *Royal Commission*, op. cit., p.70, lines, 2724-28. Sinn, *Power & Charity*, op. cit., pp.108-9, mentions that coffins were placed on emigrant ships to prevent the dead being thrown over board.

[250] *Tung Wah News*, (東華新報), 20 August 1898, p.4.

[251] 'Chinese Section of General Cemetery', Rookwood Cemetery, Anglican Trust: Register of Burials in the Necropolis at Haslem's Creek, under the Necropolis Act of 1867, 31st Victoria, no.14.

[252] 'Chinese Section of General Cemetery', op. cit., various.

[253] NAA: SP42/1; C47/2369, Wellington Wing Ning, Charles Wong Wing Kau, statutory declaration by Ah Ching, December 1914.

[254] 'Chinese Section of General Cemetery', op. cit., Ah Chung, 1892 & Ah Sing, 1884.

[255] 'Chinese Section of General Cemetery', op. cit., Ah Chung, 1889.

[256] 'Chinese Section of General Cemetery', op. cit., Rookwood has other 'Chinese Sections' which contain later burials and Sydney had at least 3-4 other cemeteries where *huaqiao* may have been buried, though Rookwood was certainly the major location. Evidence to the Chinese Gambling Commissioners was that 500 bones (from NSW?) had been sent in 'the last 10 years'. *Royal Commission*, op. cit., p.14, line, 485. In the same period 250 bones were exhumed from Rookwood.

257 *Royal Commission*, op. cit.,. cit., p.153, line, 6094. Photo by author taken in the Old Chinese Section, Rookwood Cemetery, Sydney, March 1998.

258 Sinn, *Power & Charity*, op. cit., p.18, says concern for the dead was, 'a keystone of community leadership and influence'.

259 Membership book in possession of the Tiy Loy & Co., sighted by the author.

260 *Royal Commission*, op. cit., p.15, lines, 486-7 and p.57, line, 2232.

261 *Royal Commission*, op. cit., p.105, line, 4169, 'they send some money to the Chinese Hospital in Hong Kong, the Tong Wah Yee Yuen'. Sinn, *Power & Charity*, op. cit., p.6, refers to general *huaqiao* links, p.71, n.119, mentions links with Sydney in 1887 and p.73, refers to membership by Australian organisations.

262 Figures from, Barry York, *Admitted: 1901 to 1946. Immigrants and Others Allowed into Australia between 1901 and 1946*, Centre for Immigration & Multicultural Studies, Australian National University, 1993, throughout.

263 Choi, op. cit., p.42.

264 Figures derived from Commonwealth Census data in Palfreeman, op. cit., p.145, Table III; and Choi, op. cit., p.42.

265 See, NAA: C4203/1; Boarding Branch Records, 1914-1931, vol.2, p.358, circular, Secretary to Collector of Customs, 6 September 1920, 2 July 1924 and p.449, 24 November 1926.

266 Yarwood, op. cit., p.105, states it was rare for people on certificates to be released from their conditions.

267 Yarwood, op. cit., p.112, states that the very first was on 1 April 1902 and was in fact a girl. Only three girls in total entered Australia under this category.

268 NAA: SP42/1; C11/2756, Yut Ming.

269 NAA: SP1122/1; N1953/24/2504, Lee Man Dick (Man Duck), memo, 18 February 1931.

270 Cliff Lee, 28/9/97 (4) and Wilton, op. cit., p.122, on the significance of student sponsorship.

271 Yarwood, op. cit., pp.110-112, on the evolution of the substitute and assistant categories.

272 NAA: SP42/2; C16/4361, Kee Ching.

273 NAA: SP1122/1; N57/2190, Wong Ka Yee, letter, Assistant Secretary to Wing Sang & Co., 9 April 1930.

274 Choi, op. cit., p.53, on the treatment of cabinet makers and the impact of *huaqiao* aging on the market gardens.

[275] NAA: SP1122/1; N65/3278, Lee Bing Hoong (Lee Bing Hong), letter, NSW Chamber of Fruit and Vegetable Industries to Commonwealth Migration Officer, Department of Immigration, 20 May 1952.

[276] Yarwood, op. cit., pp.110-112, on firms such as Wing On & Co. being favoured; Fitzgerald, op. cit., pp.37-40, on the need to be importer/exporters; Wilton, op. cit., pp.120-5, on the sponsorship of assistants by stores in northern NSW.

[277] NAA: SP11/12; Louey Kee Fung, report, Investigations Officer to Secretary, 31 March 1933.

[278] NAA: SP42/1; N59/3386, Kwong War Chong & Co. Figures attached to minute, 18 March 1948.

[279] Wilton, op. cit., pp.129-30, mentions this virtual bonding; Choi, op. cit., pp.86-87, on the union contribution to restricting opportunities for improvement.

[280] NAA: SP11/12; Yuk Kwan, Tai Moon, & others, 1926-47 and SP1122/1; N56/6446, Yuk Kwan Wong.

[281] NAA: SP42/1; C1903/2582, Sing Kee, letter from Collector of Customs, 6 April 1903.

[282] NAA: C4203/1; Boarding Branch Records, 1914-1931, vol.2, p.254, telegram, Secretary to Administrator, Rabaul, 19 July 1921. See Yarwood, op. cit., pp.75-7, on High Court decisions regarding children raised overseas.

[283] NAA: C4203/1; Boarding Branch Records, 1914-1931, vol.2, p.404, letter, Acting Secretary to Collector of Customs, 14/5/25.

[284] NAA: SP42/1; Choy See Pan Kee (Mrs Thomas Pan Kee), letter, Collector of Customs to Wing On, 26 June 1926.

[285] NAA: SP1122/1; N67/4101, Kwok Pearl (Mrs) (Pearl Lock Lee), letters, Collector of Customs to Kwong War Chong, 15 September 1949 and 8 February 1950.

[286] Interview with Victor Gow, 30 October 1997 (2).

[287] NAA: SP1122/1; N53/24/2298, Shelia Gock Ming, letter, Secretary to Director of Wing On, 19 March 1935.

[288] NAA: C4203/1; Boarding Branch Records, 1914-1931, vol.2, p.281, circular Secretary to Collector of Customs, 29 July 1920 and p.179, Secretary to Collector of Customs, 16 October 1919.

[289] NAA: SP1148/2; Passenger lists, Outgoing 1902, 1929, 1939. No women, apart from a very few *huaqiao* wives from Tonga, travelled in steerage.

[290] NAA: SP42/1; C11/502, Billy Chee Hoon.

[291] NAA: SP1122/1; N1952/24/3951, John Louie Hoon.

[292] NAA: C4203/1; Boarding Branch Circulars, 1914-1931, p.207, circular, Secretary to Collector of Customs, 9 June 1923.

[293] Fitzgerald, op. cit., pp.41-42, on Chinese seamen deserting their ships. Interview with Victor Gow, 30 October 1997 (7) and NAA: SP1122/1; N67/4101, Kwok Pearl (Mrs) (Pearl Lock Lee).

[294] NAA: SP42/1; C47/2352, Leong Hoi Cheng, memo, 24 January 1945.

[295] NAA: SP726/1; Particulars of Applications for CEDTs, vol. 6, 20/8/34 - 22/1/1959. See Appendix IV, Table 10.

[296] Interview with Victor Gow, 30 October 1997 (7). Sinn, *'Xin Xi Guxiang',* op. cit., p.382, Hong Kong's population was 1.6m when the Japanese invaded and 500-600,000 in 1945. The Japanese encouraged return to home districts.

[297] Interview with Billy Gay, 19 March 1998 (Tape 1, B, 200).

[298] Interview with Billy Gay, 19 March 1998 (Tape 1, B, 200).

[299] C. H. Wu, *Dollars Dependents and Dogma; o/seas Chinese remittances to Communist China,* The Hoover Institution on War, Revolution and Peace, Stanford, California, 1967, p.81, 'there were virtually no remittances … and most of the dependents lived in areas occupied by the Japanese'.

[300] Interview with Arthur Gar Lock Chang, 28 October 1997 (8). See, Wilton, op. cit., pp.221-229, on the impact of war for some families.

[301] Interview with Norman Lee, 25 September 1997 (6).

[302] Stephen Fitzgerald, op. cit., p.27, n.56. Interview with Norman Lee, 25 September 1997 (6).

[303] Wilton, op. cit., pp.229-230, on the lessening of the sense of China as home and p.232, on the effects of Australia becoming less racist.

[304] Sui, op. cit., p.107, on post-war chaos in Hong Kong; Wilton, op. cit., pp.227-8, refers to the harsh conditions and begging letters from relatives in China; Palfreeman, op. cit., p.152, Table XII gives figures on the increase in this category after the war.

[305] Interview with Arthur Gar Lock Chang, 7 March 1998 (Tape 2, A, 19.00) and Donald Young, 11 October 1998 (9).

[306] Cliff Lee, 28 September 1997 (4) & NAA: SP1122/1; N1953/24/2504, Lee Man Dick (Man Duck).

[307] NAA: SP1122/1; N52/24/1534, Young Sing.

[308] NAA: SP1122/1; N58/4695, Sun Lee.

[309] Cliff Lee, 28 September 1997 (4).

[310] Victor Gow, 30 October 1997 (11).

[311] Billy Gay, 19 March 1998 (Tape 1, B, 300).

Conclusion

[312] NAA: SP1122/1; N1953/24/2375, Lee Man Dick (Man Duck), file note 1956.

[313] See Introduction, 'An Australian Citizen Apparently'.

[314] NAA: SP42/1; C13/734, Jang See, file note, J. T. T. Donohoe, 4 December 1908.

Appendices

[315] 'Treatment of them [Chinese languages] as mere dialects is based on the fact that they all can be put down, at least to some degree, in Chinese characters acceptable to the Great Tradition.' Moser, op. cit., p.3.

[316] NAA: SP42/1; C36/813, Lily Lee (Lily Lee Ung Land), letter, Philip Lee Chun to the Collector of Customs, 1 February 1915.

[317] NAA: SP1122/1; N1952/24/3951, John Louis (Louie) Hoon. This was how Norman Lee explained the various renderings in Chinese characters of John Louie Hoon's name that appear throughout his file, interview with Norman Lee, 25 September 1997 (12).

[318] NAA: SP11/12; Yuk Kwan, Tai Moon, & others, 1926-47 and SP1122/1; N56/6446, Yuk Kwan Wong.

[319] NAA: SP726/2; Particulars of Applications for CEDTs, vol. 2, 10/1/11 - 21/10/18. For a similar explanation for the number of 'Ah' names see, Char, op. cit., p.61, n.19.

[320] NAA: SP42/1; C36/813, Lily Lee (Lily Lee Ung Land), letter Philip Lee Chun to the Collector of Customs, 1 February 1915.

[321] Census of the Commonwealth of Australia, 1911, 1921, 1933 and 1947. Official Year Book of the Commonwealth of Australia, No.18, 1925, Commonwealth Bureau of Census and Statistics, Melbourne, 1925; *Royal Commission,* op. cit., p.402; Coghlan, op. cit., p.594, Table no. 5, 'Populations in Divisions at the Census of 1891'. Also based on the Census material, Palfreeman, op. cit., p.145, Table III and Choi, op. cit., p.42, Table 3.1.

[322] Choi, op. cit., pp.78-9.

[323] Price, op. cit., p.220, n.12.

[324] Noel Butlin Archives Centre (ANU); Deposit 111, 111/2/3, Chinese Chamber of Commerce of NSW and other Chinese Associations, miscellaneous 1913-26, membership list.

[325] *Royal Commission*, op. cit., p.146, lines, 5871-2, where it is transcribed as 'Chang Sing'.

[326] *Royal Commission*, op. cit., p.54, lines, 2056-83.

[327] *Royal Commission*, op. cit., p.153, lines, 6098-99.

[328] *Royal Commission*, op. cit., p.391, lines, 14174-76 and p.145, lines, 5807-09.

[329] An interesting exception to this is during the 1930s when a question concerning the 'location of wife' was asked, the answer often given was the name of a specific village.

[330] *Royal Commission*, op. cit., p.398, line, 14490.

215

ACKNOWLEDGEMENTS

This work could not have been produced without the support, assistance and tolerance of my wife Mei-Su Chen, a tolerance stretched to breaking point and beyond on many occasions by me in the course of writing. Thanks also goes to the recently arrived Teagan Williams-Chen for her inspiring me to get it done so as to leave more time to pay her the attention she is due. Many thanks are also due to my parents for providing a quiet refuge so that this could happen.

Any researcher into oral history is always deeply indebted to those who are interviewed for their patience and their willingness to reveal so much of their lives. In this case my admiration and respect for those people of Chinese origin who survived so much goes to Arthur Gar-Lock Chang, Victor Gow, Donald Young, Norman Lee, Billy Gay, and to Cliff Lee. I especially thank Cliff Lee for his accommodating me in Zhongshan and showing me his and other *huaqiao* villages. I still dream of Cantonese food.

For his assistance in navigating the great many files in the National Archives of Australia (NAA) which provided the core evidence of this work, my thanks to archivist Paul Wood. Paul showed limitless patience as I requested file after file and box after box, 'just to see what might turn up'. Similar patience was shown by Chen Di Qiu, of the Overseas Chinese Affairs Office of Zhongshan, for allowing me access to their library, for answering my many questions and conducting me on a grand tour of the major *huaqiao* districts of the Pearl River Delta.

I offer special thanks to Dr James Hayes for his generosity in providing me with valuable and interesting contacts in Hong Kong. Dr Elizabeth Sinn of the University of Hong Kong was most helpful, particularly in making me aware of the significance of the Tung Wah Hospital in the lives of Australia's *huaqiao*.

I would also like to thank Derrick Williams, King Fong, Dr Shirley Fitzgerald and Dr Charles Price. Derrick Williams of the Anglican Trust for his generosity in granting access to the records of the Chinese Section of Rookwood Cemetery; King Fong for his providing the files of the Say Tin Co. rental receipts; Dr Shirley Fitzgerald for her assistance in making contact with members of Sydney's Chinese community; and Dr Charles Price for his explanation of his research into Sydney's *huaqiao* proportions by district of origin and for his generosity in loaning me some of his research material.

For proof reading at short notice, I wish to thank Janice Hogg. I hope that she did not find it too much of an ordeal.

The final word of thanks must go to my long suffering but always optimistic supervisor, Dr Janis Wilton, a tireless corrector of my hapless command of the English language and an insightful but subtle suggester of better ways. I have been fortunate in having as my supervisor one of the few scholars in Australia to have explored the significance of the Australia-China link.

As must always be said, because it is always true, despite the generous support and assistance of the above people, all the errors of this work are entirely my own.

About the author

Michael Williams, formerly Adjunct Professor at the Institute for Australian and Chinese Arts and Culture (IAC), Western Sydney University, is a scholar of Chinese-Australian history and a founding member of the Chinese-Australian Historical Society. He is the author of *Returning Home with Glory* (HKU Press, 2018), *Australia's Dictation Test: The test it was a Crime to Fail* (Brill, 2021) and *Every requisite for a campaign upon the gold-fields* (Chidestudy Press, 2024).

His website: Chinese Australian History in 88 Objects was shortlisted for the 2022 Premiers Digital History Prize. Michael is currently Project Manager of the *Scattered Legacy* project, a national database of Chinese Australian history.

Basic introduction to Chinese-Australian history

While there is much written on Chinese people in Australia, much of it is outdated or based on stereotypes. In the last 20 years or so a great deal of new research has added a great deal of value to our understanding. However, there is still no one standard work that covers all of this history in any useful manner.

Listed below is a selection of excellent works that together cover a broad range of this history. Anyone of these well researched pieces will help you cut through the stereotypes that continue to predominate this history.

On women
Kate Bagnall, 'Rewriting the history of Chinese families in
    nineteenth-century Australia', *Australian Historical
    Studies*, vol. 42, no. 1, March 2011: pp.62–77.

On radicalism
Gregor Benton, "Australia", pp.72-91 in *Chinese Migrants and
    Internationalism: Forgotten Histories, 1917–1945*
    (Rutledge, 2007).

On the environment
Sheng Fei, "Environmental Experiences of Chinese People in the
    Mid-Nineteenth Century Australian Gold Rushes,"
    Global Environment, 2011, 7/8: 111.

On politics
John Fitzgerald, *Big White Lie,* Sydney: UNSW Press, 2007.

On the North
Natalie Fong, The Significance of the Northern Territory in the
    Formulation of 'White Australia' Policies, 1880–1901,
    Australian Historical Studies, 49:4, 2018, pp.527-545.

On business
Peter Gibson, "Australia's Bankrupt Chinese Furniture
Manufacturers, 1880–1930", *Australian Economic
History Review*, 2018, 58: pp.87-107.

On merchants
Mei-fen Kuo, *Making Chinese Australia: Urban Elites,
Newspapers and the Formation of Chinese Australian
Identity, 1892–1912* (Clayton, Victoria: Monash
University Publishing 2013).

On North Queensland
Cathie May, *Topsawyers: The Chinese in Cairns 1870–1920*,
(Townsville: James Cook University Press, 1984).

On miners
Barry McGowan, "The Economics and Organisation of Chinese
Mining in Colonial Australia", *Australian Economic
History Review*, 2005, 45: pp.119-138.

On the villages of origin
Michael Williams, *Returning Home with Glory: Chinese
Villagers around the Pacific, 1849 to 1949* (Hong Kong:
Hong Kong University Press, 2018).

On coolie myths
Sophie Loy-Wilson, "Coolie alibis: Seizing gold from Chinese
miners in New South Wales", *International Labor and
Working Class History,* 2017, 91, pp.28-45.

On Chinese Australian literature
Wong Shee Ping, (Ely Finch, trans), *The Poison of Polygamy - A
Social Novel*, University of Sydney Press, 2019.

On oral history
Mavis Yen, (Siaoman Yen & Richard Horsburgh, eds), *South
Flows the Pearl,* (Sydney University Press, 2022).

On being a classic
C. F. Yong, *The New Gold Mountain: the Chinese in Australia,
1901- 1921* (Richmond, S. Aust: Raphael Arts, 1977).

Also available at *ChideStudy Press*

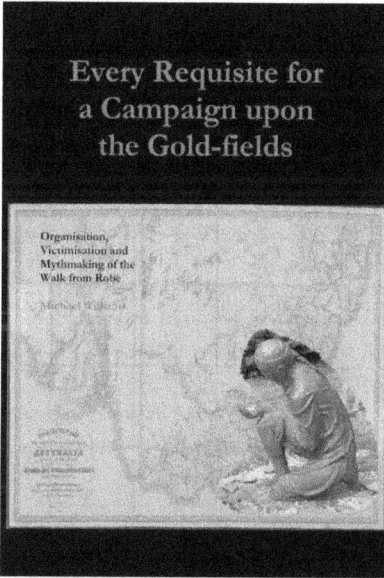

Of the many episodes that make up the oftentimes exotic impression of Chinese Australian history the 1850s walk from the small port of Robe in South Australia to the goldfields of Victoria has repeatedly taken on epic proportions. Its 'long march' like length, tales of hardship and death, not to mention present-day outrage at the discriminatory tax the walk was designed to avoid, all combine to make the stuff of legends.

Yet remarkably the telling of this history has largely been left to local historians with their characteristic eagerness to retell every tale and make use of every allusion to their subject with little regard to plausibility, contradiction or even relevance. Thus, while the arrival of thousands of gold seekers from southern China in the mid-1850s at Robetown on Guichen Bay, South Australia, in order to avoid taxes imposed by the neighbouring gold rich colony of Victoria is well known, it is surprisingly little understood in detail.

Observers 8 – Vol 1 in the **Pieces of 8** series

Having read what Chinese Australian's had to say about Chinese Australians now is your chance to read what European Australian had to say about them.

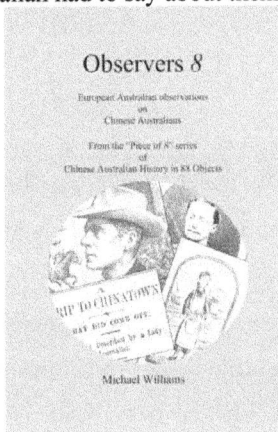

Observers 8

European Australian observations
on
Chinese Australians

From the "Pieces of 8" series
of
Chinese Australian History in 88 Objects

A TRIP TO CHINATOWN

Michael Williams

The selections range from the comments of a naive English teacher to those of an experienced China consul. From eyewitness to the arrival of the first 150 Chinese gold seekers to pass through Bathurst in 1855, as well as the astonished spectator to a Chinese opera. Not to mention the creations of the authors of both *Mary Poppins* and *The Man from Snowy River*. Of course, these sections would not be complete with reports from one each of those instant experts – the journalist and the travel writer.

Together these 'Observers 8' provide a fascinating insight into some of the many facets of Chinese Australian history.

Contents

About ChideStudy Press

Purpose
ChideStudy Press is an independent publisher designed to bridge the gap between academic publishers (too expensive and too often located behind firewalls) and popular or trade publishers (too frightened of footnotes and too willing to compromise on content).

Website

https://chidestudypresscom.wordpress.com

Email
chidestudypress@gmail.com

If you don't want to buy a copy for yourself
why not recommend that your local library buy one
for you!

www.ingramcontent.com/pod-product-compliance
Lightning Source LLC
Chambersburg PA
CBHW031953040426
42448CB00006B/345